FUTUREPROOF
YOUR GARDEN

FUTUREPROOF
YOUR GARDEN

Environmentally sustainable ways
to grow more with less

ANGUS STEWART & EMMA STEWART

murdoch books
Sydney | London

CONTENTS

◆

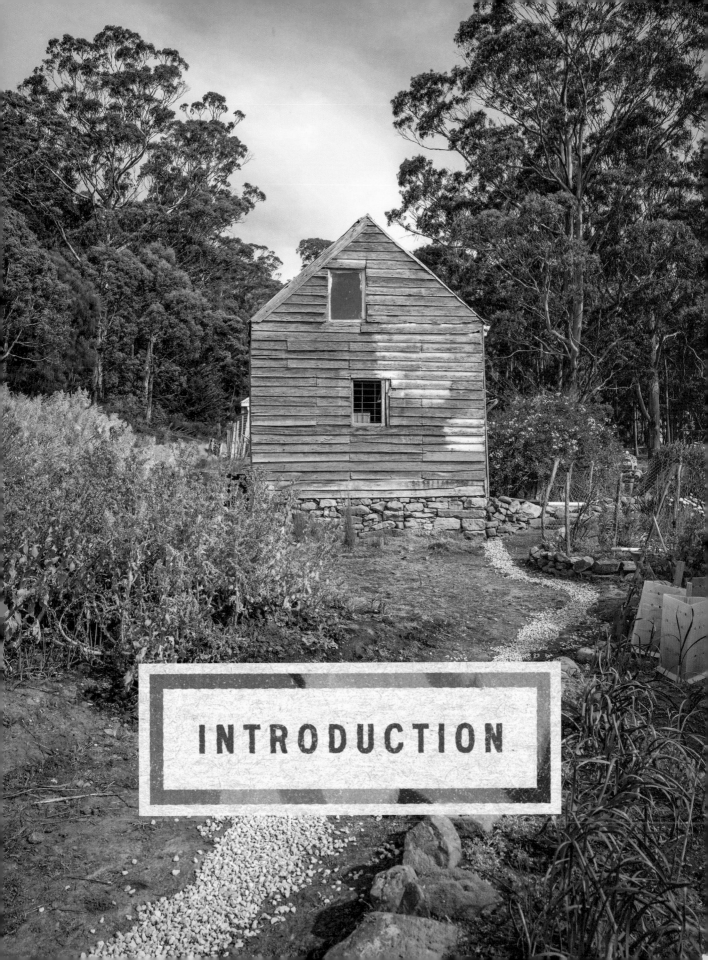

INTRODUCTION

Even though water is all around us, circulating through the environment, there is a fair chance that we take this simple and ubiquitous molecule for granted. When two atoms of hydrogen attach to one atom of oxygen, it creates an enormously versatile molecule that is important for plant growth and therefore for our existence on the planet.

Not only do water molecules act as the medium for carrying mineral nutrients from the soil to every part of the plant, but they are also chemically rearranged within the plant to supply the hydrogen and oxygen atoms that form crucial building blocks for various complex molecules. These are the end result of the solar energy captured by the plant during photosynthesis.

Without very careful management of the available reserves of water, the capacity of Earth to support an ever-increasing human population will become a problem of epic proportions. The good news is that we have the knowledge and technologies to be part of Mother Nature's endless and sustainable water cycle, which has nourished life on Earth for billions of years. We are just beginning to understand how factors such as climate change are impacting our water resources, and we can make a choice to do something about the situation. For people in many parts of the world, becoming better at managing water is a matter of life or death.

In Australia, the issue of water management is as compelling as anywhere on the planet, particularly given the dire forecasts by climate scientists. Of course, there are dissenting opinions on the trajectory of our climate into the future; however, the facts of the recent past show a clear trend for the southern half of Australia, where the vast majority of our population lives. The website of Western Australia's Department of Primary Industries and Regional Development, for instance, states that rainfall in the enormous south-western wheat-belt region has declined by around 20 per cent over just the last 50 years. The continuing controversy over irrigation water being siphoned from the Murray–Darling River system in south-eastern Australia also clearly demonstrates the need for ever-increasing action to ensure that we maximise the efficiency of our water use.

On the bright side of the water issue in Australia is the fact that our continent has been steadily drying out for many millions of years, and the Australian flora has adapted to this gradually changing climate – making native plants extremely water efficient. Not only can we use Australian plants to make a wildlife-friendly habitat for our local fauna, but we can also create gardens that need little to no irrigation. Of course, there are also many other water-efficient plants from other continents, such as cacti, that you can add to your garden-planting palette if you are looking for different forms and textures.

THE FUTUREPROOF GARDEN

In a world where our climate is changing before our very eyes, it is obvious that as well as taking measures to mitigate climate change, we also need to **adapt** to it at the same time. One of the key things climate scientists are telling us is that weather events such as droughts will occur more frequently in the future, so learning how to grow more plants with less water is an obvious place to start when it comes to futureproofing your garden. And let's not forget the challenge that

Many Australian native plants – such as lemon-scented myrtle (*Darwinia citriodora*) – provide water-smart planting options for futureproofing your garden.

too much water can bring thanks to devastating floods – we reveal how to deal with that terrible circumstance as well. This is a book about making your garden more productive and resilient, regardless of the climatic conditions that arise in the next decades.

The multitude of waterwise plants from around the globe have all evolved in their own ways to give those species the genetic potential to adapt to dry growing conditions. By selecting these plants, we are lessening not only the need for irrigation water, but also the considerable cost of creating the infrastructure – such as dams, water tanks, pipes and fittings – required to deliver water to plants. This is one of the two key approaches to water-smart gardening that this book will feature.

The second approach relates to plants that are not so well adapted to dry conditions. We are chiefly talking about fruit and vegetable species, but there are also many stunning ornamental plants that we may want to grow for their aesthetic appeal in the garden or for their cut flowers and foliage. These are the high-performance plants that will never reach their full potential if they are forced to grow without sufficient access to water. We will explore simple technologies, such as wicking beds, which allow these water-hungry plants to drink their fill without our precious high-quality irrigation water being lost to run-off and evaporation.

Farmers around the world are constantly exploring and implementing new methods and technologies to maximise water efficiency. We will give you hands-on practical information about how to adapt this knowledge for home gardens of all sizes, from tiny inner-city balconies and suburban blocks to multi-hectare hobby farms and everything in between.

As well as new ideas, we will also discuss the time-honoured ways that farmers and gardeners have maximised their water efficiency over the thousands of years of human civilisation. For instance, building your soil's capacity for storing water can be as simple and cost effective as learning to turn all of your kitchen scraps into compost or worm castings that will act like a water-storing sponge in your soil or potting mix.

We will also look at water quality and how to maintain it at a standard suitable for the

plants you are growing. You will discover how to catch and store as much water as possible from rainfall and/or town water supplies, saving anything that would otherwise go to waste as stormwater run-off. This will increase the amount of irrigation water available for growing your own food and other plants that need a lot of water to not only survive, but also thrive.

We love growing plants, and we want to show you how to do this in the most sustainable way possible, both environmentally and economically.

Happy gardening!

Angus and Emma

1

A DROP
IN THE
BUCKET

Given the overall abundance of water in rivers, lakes and oceans, it is easy to take for granted all of the things it does to sustain life on our planet. The average plant is made up of around 90 per cent water, and therefore plant life is totally reliant on water for its survival. In turn, animal life is dependent on the availability of plants for its survival.

Water (H_2O) plays a key role in supplying the hydrogen and oxygen that plants use as building blocks for the almost limitless diversity of organic molecules – such as proteins, carbohydrates, fats and oils – that are so important to us animals as sources of food, fibre and medicine. Those simple building blocks of hydrogen and oxygen are bound with carbon from carbon dioxide (CO_2) and various essential mineral elements to form incredible molecular combinations.

But it doesn't stop there. Water is also essential for both holding plants upright and keeping the breathing pores in the leaves (stomata) open to allow photosynthesis to occur. At the same time, water carries mineral nutrients from the soil into the plant.

DROUGHTS AND FLOODS

A deficit of water quickly leads to the phenomenon we all recognise as wilting. Have you ever wondered why you only see it in the shoot tips of plants? Why tall trees don't wilt in a drought? The answer lies in the woody reinforcing tissues that some perennial plants build up during their life. Herbaceous plants such as annuals – think pansies and primulas – have no woody tissue at all and, accordingly, severe water stress in these plants results in the rather dramatic collapse that we all recognise on very hot days. However, woody plants such as trees can suffer just as dramatically when deprived of water for an extended period. Soil scientists refer to an extremely dry soil as being

at **permanent wilting point**, and there are dire consequences for any plants growing in it. This is the point at which there is no water available for uptake by plants, and it will usually lead to the death of the plants.

When a particular soil becomes saturated with water – say, during a storm – then literally all available spaces (pores) in the soil become filled with water that cannot drain away fast enough. Eventually, when the rain stops, much of the water in the saturated pore spaces drains through the soil thanks to gravity. The water that is left behind is bound to soil particles, and the soil is then holding the maximum possible amount of water against the force of gravity. Plant roots are able to exert enough suction to be able to use the moisture that is stuck to the soil particles, and hence this is the water available for uptake by plants. This soil state is called **field capacity**. So, between field capacity and permanent wilting point, we have a reservoir of water available for uptake by plants. We will revisit this subject in Chapter 4 when we talk about ways to improve this all-important reservoir of moisture that your plants simply cannot live without.

When soils are subjected to prolonged rainfall events, they become waterlogged. Paradoxically, plants growing in these saturated soils can be susceptible to wilting – not because the plants are too dry, but because the wet conditions cause the root system to stop functioning, or even rot. The plants can no longer take up water, even though they are literally surrounded by a sea of it!

This eastern spinebill is pollinating a kangaroo paw (*Anigozanthos* species) in a water-smart wildlife-habitat garden.

As the world's population increases, we must become more conservative with our water usage.

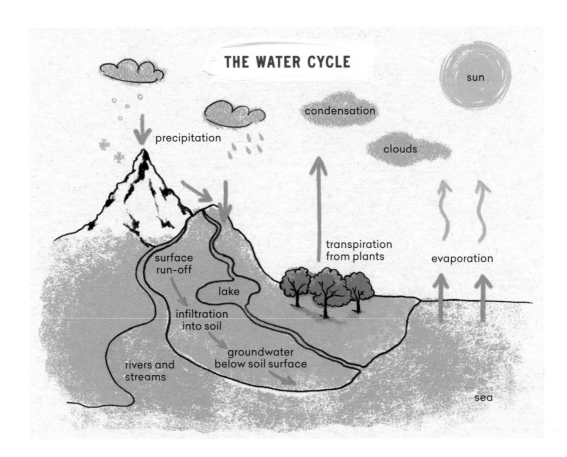

THE WATER CYCLE

(diagram labels: sun, condensation, clouds, precipitation, transpiration from plants, evaporation, surface run-off, lake, infiltration into soil, groundwater below soil surface, rivers and streams, sea)

Ensuring that your garden soil is able to drain away excess water in the most environmentally friendly way possible is almost as vital as improving the water-holding capacity of the soil.

One of the most commonly used expressions in gardening books is that a particular plant needs a soil with perfect drainage, but one that also stores plenty of moisture for plant growth. At first glance, this statement seems to be contradictory. However, it will make sense once we show you how to build your soil's water-holding capacity in a way that also ensures excess moisture can drain away as stormwater during a major rainfall event. If we can achieve this 'holy grail' of gardening, then we will have gone a long way to creating a soil that will suit an extremely wide range of plant species.

THE WATER CYCLE

The amount of water on the planet remains fairly constant throughout time, so we can refer to water as a finite resource. This is readily apparent during periods of drought, when running out of water can be lethal not only for your garden but also for the life it supports. However, how do we explain the fact that, when the drought breaks, we suddenly seem to have plenty of water again and everyone relaxes their behaviour, because it feels like there will always be an endless supply of water?

The answer to this apparent paradox is the concept of the water cycle – sometimes known as the hydrological cycle – which describes the continuous movement of water on, above and below Earth's surface. Science tells us that although the amount of water on Earth is relatively constant, its distribution across the planet varies on a day-to-day basis. Understanding the water cycle helps us to manage the various processes that are within our control, which in turn allows us to maintain both water supply and – perhaps just as importantly – water quality.

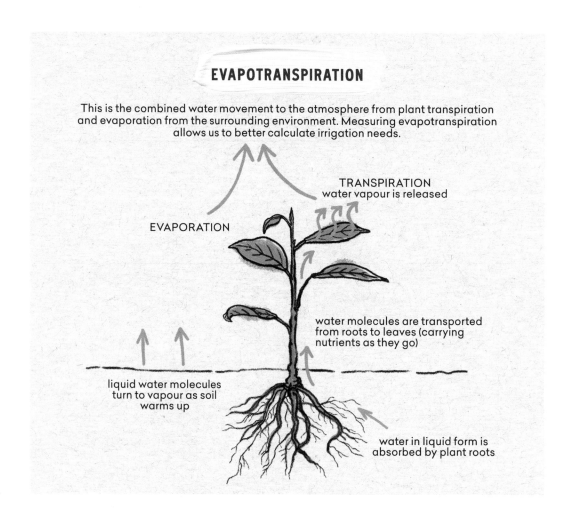

EVAPOTRANSPIRATION

This is the combined water movement to the atmosphere from plant transpiration and evaporation from the surrounding environment. Measuring evapotranspiration allows us to better calculate irrigation needs.

TRANSPIRATION
water vapour is released

EVAPORATION

water molecules are transported from roots to leaves (carrying nutrients as they go)

liquid water molecules turn to vapour as soil warms up

water in liquid form is absorbed by plant roots

Rain, rain, everywhere ...

The water that falls from the sky is one of those priceless commodities that we are given for free but often take for granted until, of course, there is a drought. As well as rain, there are various other forms that this heavenly gift can take: hail, snow, sleet and drizzle. The collective term for water that comes from the sky is **precipitation**. It results from the condensation of atmospheric water vapour, which then falls from clouds due to the force of gravity. Generally speaking, we have very little control over this precious process, although there have been experiments with cloud seeding that have had some success. However, precipitation is not something that the average gardener can conjure up when a likely looking cloud passes overhead.

The reverse process to precipitation is **evaporation**, a concept we are all too familiar with as we sweat our way through a blazing summer's day. If the humidity is not too high, the process of evaporation causes our sweat to vaporise, which in turn cools our skin and body. The evaporation rate on any given day is determined by three main variables: temperature, humidity and wind speed.

While we are talking about evaporation, we also need to understand the parallel process of **transpiration**, which results from the movement of water within plants from the roots to the leaves, where the water molecules become vapour that transpires from the leaf pores (stomata) to the atmosphere. The vital thing to understand about plant growth is that if transpiration stops when a plant becomes water-stressed, then growth stops and the plant will not realise its full potential with regard to growth rate. The twin concepts of evaporation and transpiration are often

ENERGY EXCHANGE

When perspiration evaporates from our skin, heat energy is absorbed by the surrounding air – resulting in a cooling effect. In the same way, the process of transpiration results in the cooling of plant leaves. This is critical to a plant's survival in extreme heat, because unlike us, plants cannot move and avoid the sun to cool themselves. On the flipside, when water vapour condenses into droplets on a plant's surface (such as on leaves), heat is released. This warming effect can be critical in limiting the damage done by frosts on a cold winter's morning.

Left: The change of water from solid to liquid to gas involves an energy exchange that we can use to our advantage in the garden.

considered together as **evapotranspiration**, which is the sum of evaporation and plant transpiration from a given area, helping us to estimate irrigation requirements. When water evaporates or transpires from a surface, that water is purified as it goes back into the atmosphere and thus the cycle continues, replenishing Earth's surface with pure water.

The good news for gardeners is that, unlike with precipitation levels, we can have an enormous influence over evapotranspiration through our various gardening practices. We can control the rate of evaporation from our water-storage facilities (for example, by storing this precious liquid in covered tanks rather than in open ponds or dams) and – most importantly – from the soil surface, through the use of mulches or subsurface (capillary) watering. We can also have plenty of say over transpiration if our water supply is limited and we need to ration it to our plants. For example, ornamental plants in a shrubbery can be 'shut down' by gradually acclimatising them to less irrigation water over time, in a way that does not cause catastrophic damage to the plant.

Two other critical parts of the water cycle are **infiltration** of water into the soil, and **surface run-off** that results in the formation of watercourses, such as creeks and rivers. Again, as gardeners, we can have a great influence over these two processes to benefit the plants that we want to grow. If we ensure that the infiltration rate is optimal for our soil type, then we can maximise the storage of water in our soil's pore spaces so it is available to be used by plants. Studying and redirecting surface run-off where it is appropriate to do so allows us to harvest water and store it in the soil or in tanks and dams.

THE WATER CYCLE AND CLIMATE CHANGE

Throughout the history of agriculture, humanity has caused deserts to form when land has been cleared of vegetation. By re-establishing forests on vacant land, we can change the water cycle on a localised basis and reverse the process of desertification.

Using mulch such as pine bark helps to stop water evaporating from the soil surface.

Gardens all over Europe relied on gravity-fed water supplies in the absence of machinery.

SUPPLYING WATER TO YOUR GARDEN

The development of technologies for water storage and movement is one of the key things that has enabled humans to create horticulture, agriculture and civilisation. Ancient remnants of these incredibly sophisticated technologies can be found all over the world, perhaps best exemplified by the Roman aqueducts that moved water over long distances – sometimes many kilometres – using only gravity to make it happen. Gardens all over Europe relied on gravity-fed water supplies in the absence of machinery. In modern times, massive dams are used to store water in vast volumes that can then be transported to urban users via a system of underground pipes.

Urban environments around the world usually have a secure mains supply of water that can be relied upon for irrigation. Mains water has the outstanding convenience of being readily available in virtually unlimited quantities (for the home gardener, at least), but if something goes wrong with water quality, or if quantity becomes limited by water restrictions in times of drought, then it is highly desirable to have an alternative independent water supply, such as a tank, dam or water bore (depending on your circumstances).

Harvesting fresh water to create your own independent supply – whether it is your only source of water in a remote location or as a vital backup supply – has many benefits. As well as taking the pressure off mains water supplies, you can save significant sums on your water bills and preserve community water supplies for those inevitable periods when there are not so many rainy days. At an environmental level, the enormous dams built in the twentieth century have often proven to be disastrous downstream; it is better if possible to decentralise water storage in much smaller volumes, such as ponds, farm dams and water tanks.

WATER QUALITY

The quality of water should be carefully regulated to ensure that it is **potable** (which means that it is safe for drinking or for use in preparing food). Some municipal authorities add substances to the potable water supply, such as fluoride to improve dental health, and water quality can vary over time. Mains water supplies are constantly monitored for quality, though, and it should be safe to assume that you do not need to test it yourself to ensure that it is okay to drink or to use in the garden. However, various other water-storage facilities that you install on your property will need to be maintained properly to ensure that your ongoing supply of water is fit for your intended purpose.

Water quality has two aspects: chemical (for example, salt levels) and biological (for example, the presence of animal and/or plant pathogens). Sometimes we can see contamination in the form of clay particles suspended in dam water, but more often than not, water quality is a rather tricky concept for the layperson to assess. Contaminants are often invisible and can only be measured with scientific equipment, such as a salinity meter, or identified by growing microbes in a laboratory agar plate. The equipment that is needed to discover invisible contaminants is not likely to be in the toolkit of the average suburban handyperson. If you are setting up a water-harvesting and storage system, then it is highly advisable to engage a qualified plumber or water-quality specialist to ensure the safety and quality of your water.

If you go to the trouble and expense of getting a scientific analysis of your water quality, then seek out a laboratory that will also give you recommendations about what to do if your water is not fit for its designated purpose. In particular, make sure you test for the following things:

> ## Water storage will need to be maintained properly to ensure that your ongoing supply of water is fit for your intended purpose.

Far left: A solar pumping system at Angus's local community garden in Tasmania utilises stormwater that has been stored in a dam at the lowest point on the site.

Left: While the water in the community-garden dam is not potable, it is absolutely fit for the purpose of providing supplementary irrigation water to the plants.

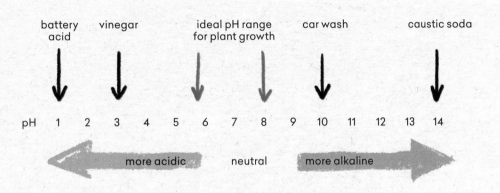

THE pH SCALE

battery acid — pH 1
vinegar — pH 3
ideal pH range for plant growth — pH 6
car wash — pH 10
caustic soda — pH 14

pH   1   2   3   4   5   6   7   8   9   10   11   12   13   14

← more acidic   neutral   more alkaline →

* **pH** – is your water acidic or alkaline? This may have both short- and long-term consequences for your garden.

* **salinity** – unfortunately, salts found in your water are not limited to common salt (sodium chloride). A wide variety of minerals qualify as salts, and when dissolved in water they can greatly alter its nutritional quality and raise its salinity. If the dissolved salts rise too high in water, they can make it too salty for plant growth and as drinking water. One option with a saline water supply is to dilute it with water from a clean supply (such as mains water) to create a mixture that is acceptable for use in the garden.

* **pathogens** – obviously, we do not want the problems caused by plant or human pathogens in the garden. If the results are positive, then we need to work out where the pathogens are coming from and either eliminate the source or treat the water to kill the pathogens. There are various water-treatment options for this purpose, but they are a rather specialist topic for which you should seek expert advice and help.

TERRIBLE TANK WATER

A few years ago, Angus was house-sitting for a friend in rural Tasmania and was thrilled to be drinking what he thought was pure rainwater collected from the roof and stored in a corrugated-iron tank. After a few weeks, he developed a consistently upset stomach (he won't go into too much detail, but it did involve a lot of running to the bathroom). A visit to the doctor and some testing revealed that he had contracted a nasty pathogen called *Salmonella* Mississippi, with the most likely source being the untreated water he was drinking.

On researching the topic, he discovered that native animals – such as the brush-tailed possum – are a reservoir of infection for this disease. As most Australians have experienced at some stage in their lives, possums love to inhabit roof cavities and come out at night, clambering across the rooftop on their way to consuming the tender young shoot tips throughout the garden. It would be miraculous if they did not leave the occasional manure calling card on the roof, and when this inevitably happens, some of this manure (and the microbes in it) finds its way into the water being collected from that roof. Since then, Angus has been particularly careful about boiling his water to ensure its 'biological safety'.

2

HARVESTING WATER

As the human population grows, there is increasing pressure on water supplies in various parts of the world. From a gardening perspective, Australia is generally regarded as the driest continent on the planet, with our changing climate causing many parts of the country to become progressively drier.

In the second half of the twentieth century, Australia began to rely on massive dams to ensure a constant water supply for urban dwellers. Thanks to this, most of us now take for granted our ability to turn on the tap and **always** see water flowing from it! Of course, there are people in other parts of the world who can only dream of such a scenario.

However, the early mentality of relying solely on a centralised water-supply system reached rather farcical proportions when many local water authorities outlawed the use of water tanks by private households, ostensibly for health reasons (such as preventing mosquitoes from breeding). Regardless, folk in rural areas where there was no mains supply happily went on using their tanks as they always had. It should be said that mosquitoes and other nasty organisms are sometimes found in poorly maintained water tanks, but our modern knowledge and technologies are such that these problems can be controlled by properly educated and resourced users. Thankfully, the anti-water-tank philosophy appears to have changed during this millennium, as officials at all government levels across Australia have acknowledged the need to shore up our dwindling water supplies in whatever ways are possible.

ARE DESALINATION PLANTS THE ANSWER?

Australia's apparently never-ending water supply has become increasingly precarious as climate change alters both the amount and distribution of precipitation, with governments in several states deciding to invest in large-scale desalination plants to supplement the dams that depend on river flows. Desalination plants work by taking salt water – usually from ocean sources (but groundwater from bores can also have salt levels that are toxic to plants) – and pushing it through various filtration processes to remove the salt and any other impurities. Most desalination plants currently rely on fossil fuel to provide their energy, a somewhat unsustainable exercise. They will become a much better solution in the near future, when they will likely switch to renewable energy sources.

Most of us take for granted our ability to turn on the tap and always see water flowing from it.

Water-tank technology is constantly improving, and there are now options for virtually every new building type.

WATER TANKS

A water tank is a great investment on several levels, because it is a way of collecting pure rainwater that can be used for any purpose – from beautiful drinking water to good-quality water for the garden. Tanks can also be used to mix liquid fertilisers – particularly organic feeds such as worm-farm leachates – and distribute them to your garden.

There are many different options when it comes to water tanks, and we will explore this topic with a view to helping you choose the right one for your situation. Gone are the days when your only option was a large corrugated-iron tank taking up valuable garden space and looking somewhat awkward next to the house. Water tanks now come in a huge range of shapes, sizes and colours so they can match their surroundings. You can even have an underground tank incorporated into a concrete slab, or a flexible water bladder that is virtually invisible sitting beneath your house or deck – just the thing for the pocket-sized blocks of land that are now so common in suburbia.

Siting your tank

One of the first decisions to make is where you will site your tank, as this will help determine its size, shape and colour (do you want it to blend in or contrast with the landscape?). Locating the tank under cover will generally lengthen its life span and keep it free from falling debris, such as leaves and sticks. Shade the tank to keep it cool, particularly in hotter climates, as this will minimise the possibility of microbes growing in your precious water source. Some well-placed shrubs, such as fast-growing wattles (*Acacia* species), are an excellent option if your buildings don't give enough shade.

If you do not have space for one large tank, you could also consider installing a network of interconnected smaller tanks. You will also need to consider whether you require mains power to move the water around your property (alternatives are solar-powered pumps, or gravity-fed water if you are on a sloping site).

Underground tanks can be a useful option on very small blocks where they can be sited

Above left:
Polyethylene water tanks are a cost-effective storage option in a wide range of situations.

Above right:
The traditional corrugated-iron tank is resistant to flames, so it is a superb choice for bushfire-prone regions.

beneath buildings or driveways. Obviously, special attention needs to be given to the tank if it has a load to bear, such as a car or truck driving over it. Concrete tanks can be fortified and even constructed on site. The logistics and costs of pumping water from an underground tank must also be considered when looking at this option.

Bladders are useful if your house or decking is mounted on stumps or piers. Depending on what the water will be used for, you may need to ensure that the bladder is made of a plastic that does not taint the water with substances such as phthalates. If you are using the water on your vegetable garden, for instance, then make sure your tank will consistently supply potable (drinkable) water.

Locating your tank in relation to the catchment roof – whether that is a house, carport or shed – is the next consideration. Putting it beside or under the structure will reduce the amount of pipework needed, but if it makes more sense to place it further away, then the added expense of the extra pipework may not be an issue. You also need to think about having access to the tank to keep it clean, both inside and outside.

Tank materials

The next question is what sort of material to use. All rainwater tanks will do the job of storing water, but your choice will be informed by your individual situation. Weigh up the pros and cons of each tank type, and see how many of your boxes it ticks.

1 **Metal tanks** come in several forms, with the main options being corrugated iron (galvanised steel), stainless steel and Aquaplate Colorbond. Slightly rusty corrugated-iron tanks are the ones most often seen throughout rural Australia. The durability and longevity of metal tanks are the big advantages, and this can lead to a life span of at least 20 years (possibly more if corrosion can be minimised). Salts of any kind are the biggest cause of corrosion, and they can come from salty water (such as that found in some bores), fertilisers or sea spray. Care must be taken not to damage the corrosion-resistant coatings on corrugated-iron or

HOW MUCH WATER CAN BE HARVESTED FROM YOUR ROOF?

To work out how big your water tank needs to be – assuming you have enough space and your budget allows – you need to calculate the maximum amount of water that is likely to be captured by your roof. Use our formula below to work out the total amount of water in a given period, such as a year. Depending on your usage patterns and the seasonality of your rainfall, you can then calculate how big your tank needs to be to catch every drop of water. Balance this with your budget and your water needs. While you may be able to harvest tens of thousands of litres, can you use all of that water? Maybe a smaller tank will satisfy your needs. However, it is worth considering that your tank water can also be used for things that don't need a potable water supply, such as flushing toilets, washing cars and, of course, growing your garden.

To calculate the total amount of water that is harvestable from your roof during the year, you'll need to know:

* the surface area of your roof = length x width (for example, 15 metres x 10 metres = 150 square metres)
* your annual rainfall in metres (for example, 1160 millimetres = 1.16 metres)
* the handy fact that 1 cubic metre of water = 1000 litres

The maximum amount of rainfall that can be harvested equals the surface area of the roof multiplied by the annual rainfall. Using the example measurements above:

= 15 metres x 10 metres x 1.16 metres
= 174 cubic metres of water
= 174,000 litres

This figure represents the total amount of water you can catch and hold on to if you have unlimited storage space in tanks or dams. You will also want to look at the **distribution** of your rainfall throughout the year. For instance, someone living in Darwin will experience both a wet season and a dry season, so any catchment will ideally have the capacity to collect most of the year's rainfall within the few months of the wet season.

Colorbond tanks, as this can be the starting point for corrosion. The Colorbond product is available in a range of colours and is lined on the inside with a waterproof membrane to prevent corrosion; corrugated-iron tanks can also be lined with zinc plating. In all cases, metal tanks provide a potable water supply. They will also survive all but the most intense bushfires.

2 **Concrete tanks** have the advantage of being able to be created on-site, which can result in considerable savings in freight costs. Because of their structural strength, they are a great option for underground storage. Concrete tanks are ideal for bushfire-prone areas as they are non-flammable. The disadvantages of concrete include its cost and heavy weight relative to other materials, as well as the fact that it can sweat if the interior of the tank is not lined with a suitable waterproof membrane.

3 **Plastic tanks** are cost-effective, relatively lightweight and quite often portable, and their availability in a range of colours and shapes makes them a practical option. They are also resistant to corrosion, and generally bounce back into shape if falling branches or other objects hit them. They are often referred to as 'poly' tanks because they are usually made of polyethylene, but they can also be made of polypropylene (which is a bit more brittle). In any case, even with the addition of ultraviolet-light inhibitors, the plastic will gradually degrade, especially if the tank is in full sun. It is also important to ensure that if your plastic tank is lined with a membrane, it does not taint your water (depending on the end use of the water). Plastic tanks are more easily damaged than those made from metal or concrete, but plastic fabricators with the right tools can easily repair them. You can patch small holes with a suitable sealant (such as 3M Scotch-Weld) from a hardware store.

GO FOR THE GOLD STANDARD

If you are going to use the water from your tank on edible plants or as drinking water, then make sure that your tank complies with relevant Australian Standards. AS/NZS 4020-2018 ensures that your tank and the other components in your rainwater-collection system do not leach into the water any chemicals that could affect the health of the consumer. This is a useful way to make certain that your system is fit for purpose. Another Australian standard that is worth looking for when purchasing plastics for use in edible gardens is AS 2070, as compliant plastic products are guaranteed to be suitable for contact with food.

As well as the variously shaped and coloured plastic tanks that are designed for permanent installation beside buildings, there is also a more portable option: **intermediate bulk containers (IBCs)**. Sometimes enclosed in a metal cage that greatly assists their durability and portability, these plastic containers generally store around 1000 litres and are often used to transport various liquids around the world. When mounted on a trailer or utility vehicle, IBCs are very handy for watering or liquid fertilising plants in dryland situations. If you are considering IBCs for your garden, check that they are made of a plastic that is suitable for your purpose (see the box on the opposite page, which discusses Australian Standards for plastics).

Installing the tank

Once you have chosen the tank that best suits your purpose, site and budget, the next step is installation. The weight of a full tank is significant, with each 1000 litres of water weighing a tonne (1000 kilograms). It is therefore important that you provide a suitably stable and level base on which your tank can sit. Depending on the tank's size, a concrete slab will provide the strongest support; however, if the soil underneath is unlikely to shrink and swell (as some clays do), then a level above-ground base comprising gravel enclosed within a raised timber edge is a low-cost alternative.

Plumbing your tank is the next consideration, and this is where hiring a suitably experienced professional (such as a plumber) is usually a worthwhile investment. It is vital that all of the fittings used to transfer the water from the catchment roof to the tank are fit for purpose. Remember, if you are planning to use the water for drinking or on edible plants, then the fittings should conform to Australian Standard AS/NZS 4020-2018.

When it comes to the pipework, there are two types of connection:

1   **A 'dry' system** is where the pipework from your guttering is all above-ground. It runs downwards from the gutter to the tank, and it drains completely between rainfall

TANKS FOR FIGHTING FIRES

The reality of global warming is that bushfires are posing an ever-increasing danger to Australians and their properties. Therefore, if you are in a fire-prone area, it is vital to store as much rainwater as possible on your property in a water tank dedicated to firefighting purposes.

The firestorms in recent times have forced changes to building codes to help mitigate the risks. An assessment known as a Bushfire Attack Level (BAL) rating is now the basis for establishing the requirements for construction (under the Australian Standard AS 3959-2009, Construction of Buildings in Bushfire-Prone Areas). The higher the rating, the greater the risk – and this will inform decisions about the installation of tanks reserved for firefighting. Indeed, in some regions your state authority may have already mandated this as a requirement for a Development Application. Even if it is not mandatory, you may choose the peace of mind of this option if you have sufficient rainfall that can be collected.

For those living in an existing property rather than building a new one, it is still an excellent idea to research the current standards and recommendations from government and firefighting authorities, especially given the increasing risks predicted by climate scientists. If you choose to have a firefighting tank, clearly mark it so it can be identified from a distance, and check that the outlet valve is compatible with firefighting tankers. These practical steps can make all the difference in an emergency situation.

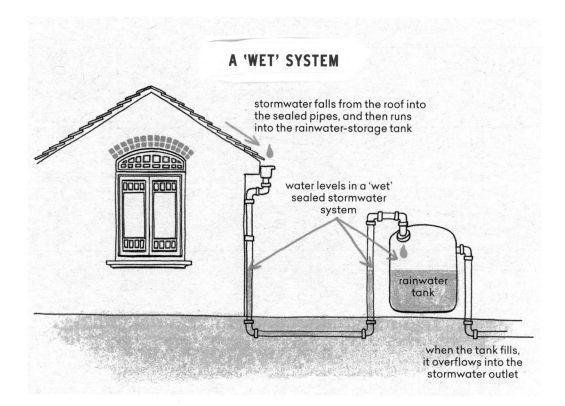

A 'WET' SYSTEM

stormwater falls from the roof into the sealed pipes, and then runs into the rainwater-storage tank

water levels in a 'wet' sealed stormwater system

rainwater tank

when the tank fills, it overflows into the stormwater outlet

events so there is no standing water in the pipework. This type of system works well when the tank is very close to the catchment roof, as the pipes can be securely fastened above the tank.

2 **A 'wet' system** is where part of the pipework from the guttering is lower than the tank and is usually buried underground. Water stays in the system between catchment events, because it has nowhere else to go. This type of system is used if the tank is on the opposite side of the building to the catchment roof, or when the tank needs to be situated away from the catchment building and you don't want long lengths of pipework suspended above the ground where they can be easily damaged. Another notable situation is when you have multiple downpipes from different sides of the building feeding water into a single tank. The 'wet' system relies on the generation of sufficient water pressure during a rainfall event to push the water up and into the tank. The

disadvantage of a 'wet' system is that long intervals between rainfall events increase the chance of the water in the pipework becoming a breeding ground for mosquitoes and collecting impurities. We can overcome this by insect-proofing the system and utilising first flush diverters (see opposite).

Other considerations with tank water

Filtering out or excluding unwanted debris – such as leaves and animal droppings – is a highly desirable objective, particularly if you will be drinking the water from the tank. Large contaminants such as fallen leaves can be excluded by using **gutter guards**, which run along the entire gutter length. Gutter guards with an appropriate mesh size and preferably made from stainless steel can also help to prevent embers from entering your gutter during a bushfire. **Rainheads** are mesh-covered buckets inserted at the top of your downpipes to divert any debris that makes its way through gutter guards (if these have been installed).

Here are some other useful tank accessories that you may want to install:

* **First flush diverters** get rid of the initial water from rainfall events, which may be contaminated by debris and sediment that has collected in your gutters and pipes during dry periods. This stops your tank's filtration system from getting clogged up. The amount of water that is diverted in that first flush will depend on the roof-catchment area. A good rule of thumb is to divert 1 litre of water for every square metre of catchment area on your roof. Consulting a specialist in this area is a good insurance policy if you are worried about making your own calculation. Some manufacturers include a first flush diverter with their tanks, but ensure that it has the capacity to deal with your roof area.

* **Pre-tank filters** have a finer filtration system than gutter guards and rainheads, and this can remove much smaller particles (such as silt and minute fragments of animal droppings). This is particularly useful if you are collecting water for drinking or for using on your vegetable garden. If you go down this path, then look for a pre-tank filter that is self-cleaning.

* **Tank-monitoring gauges** constantly measure the amount of water in tanks, and they can greatly assist efficient water use. They are particularly helpful in situations such as short-stay rental properties, where the water usage can vary enormously over short periods of time.

Filtering out unwanted debris is a desirable objective, particularly if you will be drinking water from the tank.

Above: A pre-tank filter such as a Maelstrom removes fine particles before they contaminate the water.

Left: An insect-proof tank-overflow filter prevents water contamination by pests such as mosquitoes.

A WORD ABOUT TANKS

For those without access to a mains water supply, tank water is often the only option; every time the tank is emptied, the user is reminded of how finite that supply is. On a broader scale, however, climate change and the more severe droughts that are affecting vulnerable parts of the world are also bringing home the reality that our mains water supplies are finite over any given period of time. Even though we have vast dams in various parts of Australia, our population is increasing and many people still waste copious amounts of water. It seems silly to provide very expensive potable water through the mains water supply, only to have much of that beautiful, clean water literally flushed down the toilet – especially when we can harvest water in a sustainable way to supplement mains water supplies. Rainwater tanks provide us with not only the opportunity to appreciate how long a finite water supply lasts, but also a perfect water source for the ornamental garden and other places (such as toilets) where the potability of the water is not important. That said, installing tanks and the infrastructure to service them requires a significant financial investment and is not always an option, given the spiralling cost of housing (whether that is purchasing or renting a property). Governments are starting to see the need to adapt to climate change, and it is time that we come up with schemes to subsidise the capital costs of more efficient water storage and use, in the same way that renewable energy is increasingly being funded.

RETROFITTING NEW RAINWATER-COLLECTION TECHNOLOGY

About five years ago, Angus purchased a 15-hectare farm in Tasmania that has relied on rainwater collection and a spring-fed dam for its entire hundred-year existence. As well as the original farmhouse (constructed in the 1920s), which has been extended over the years, there are several sheds around the farm that provide a ready catchment for the moderate amount of rainwater that typically falls each year. The Mediterranean climate means that most precipitation occurs in winter, and summer is usually dry, so maximising the efficiency of water collection and storage is absolutely critical to ensure that the farm doesn't run out of water during summer when demand is at its highest.

Angus decided to call in a specialist company in the field of rainwater harvest, Blue Mountain Co, to upgrade the existing infrastructure and to improve the quantity and quality of water harvested from the various buildings around the farm. Let's look at each building and the design considerations used to improve each system.

The old farmhouse.
For around a hundred years, the roof has provided drinking and household water via rainwater collection. The original roof area was greatly extended in the 1970s, which approximately doubled the catchment area of the roof to a little over 200 square metres. All water collected was originally channelled into a 23,000-litre tank via a 'wet' pipe system from the south-west corner of the house. There were two problems when it came to upgrading the system. Firstly, there was a lot of water overflowing during significant rainfall events; and secondly, organic matter from fallen leaves and from wildlife activity (birds and possums) on the roof was affecting the water quality. With an annual rainfall of approximately 600 millimetres (0.6 metres), the amount of water that could potentially be harvested is 200 square metres (roof area) x 0.6 metres (annual rainfall) = 120 cubic metres of water = 120,000 litres. Clearly, a second tank was necessary to store water during peak rainfall periods.

To improve water quality, several important measures were implemented. **Rainheads** known as Leaf Eater Original with the Hood were installed on each of the downpipes that feed the rainwater tank. These stop leaves and debris from entering the system as early as possible. The screens also secure the system from mosquitoes and other pests that can enter via downpipe connections. It was important to install the rainheads at least 500 millimetres higher than the inlet to the tank, to ensure that there was enough head pressure for the water to push through to the tank effectively.

A **first flush diverter** called First Flush Delta In-ground was installed to further improve water quality by reducing the quantity of roof contaminants entering the tank. This is particularly desirable because the water is being used for drinking and internal appliances. As the farm is in a remote rural area and the potential for airborne pollution is relatively low, Blue Mountain Co recommended diverting the first 0.5 litre per square metre of roof area. Since the roof is 200 square metres, this means diverting around 100 litres via six 1.6-metre lengths of 100-millimetre pipe. An additional pre-filter called a **Maelstrom** has been used to take out very fine particles, as its filter is five times finer than that of the rainheads. The various pre-filtering measures go a long way to eliminating contamination, and this means that downstream filtration systems installed as part of the water supply to the building fixtures will require much less maintenance and have a longer life.

The **tank-overflow outlets** are also of vital importance, especially in preventing mosquitoes from entering via the 'back door' of the tank. The number and size of the overflow outlets should be equal to or greater than the number and size of the inlets in the tank to enable excess water to efficiently exit the tank during heavy rainfall. The overflow

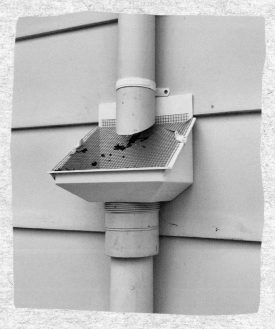

Above: Rainheads prevent coarse contaminants from entering water-storage tanks.

Maximising the efficiency of water storage is critical to ensure that the farm doesn't run out of water.

to the tank requires protection, and this can be done in a variety of ways. Angus used a Mozzie Stoppa fitted directly to the overflow outlet of the tank. Alternatively, a high-flow flap valve could be installed on the end of the overflow pipe in a stormwater pit below ground. Last but not least, a **tank-monitoring gauge** was installed in an easy-to-access location so the amount of water in the tank at any given moment can be measured.

The old dairy shed.
This building is relatively close to surrounding bushland, which poses a bushfire risk, and it is used as a multifunction space for workshop-type events on the farm – hence the water harvested from the roof is used for drinking as well as for the gardens around the building. **Gutter mesh** was installed (2-millimetre steel Blue Mountain Mesh, to comply with the Bushfire Attack Level rating of the property), which keeps small leaves, pests and bushfire embers out of the gutters and roof. A **Maelstrom** filter was installed as a pre-filter, with a Mozzie Stoppa device used on the overflow; a **tank-monitoring gauge** was also installed. The system feeds water into a 10,000-litre tank via a 'wet' system, so it is important to manage the standing water that sits in the pipes between rainfall events. Installing

a **sliding-gate valve** at the lowest point of the system allows for periodic draining of the charged water line. Draining this poorly oxygenated water from the pipes will ensure that the quality of the rest of the water is as good as it can be.

The middle shed.
This building is used for potting plants and distilling essential oils, and therefore requires relatively clean water from the 10,000-litre tank to feed the steam-distillation equipment, as well as to water plants in the adjacent nursery area. **Rainheads** and a Mozzie Stoppa device were installed, as was a **sliding-gate valve** to enable flushing of the 'wet' pipe system. Finally, a **tank-monitoring gauge** was also installed. The bottom line for this shed was that a reasonably high standard of filtration was needed but not to the very high standard of the farmhouse, where drinking water is a necessity.

Creating your own system.
Each project will be different, depending on the end purpose of the water collected. Consulting a specialist is a desirable step in order to explore all of the options. They can come up with a cost-effective system that ensures you have water quality fit for your various purposes.

Maintenance of your tank-water system

It is a good idea to inspect your entire system at least once every six months (or more often if you have the potential for lots of debris to enter your system). Check and clean your roof and gutters, and remove any overhanging branches. Tank inlets, first flush diverters and any insect-proof mesh should be cleaned and repaired if necessary.

Look inside the tank if possible, checking for any signs of incursions from insects, birds, frogs or other animals, and close up any entry points. If you see green algae growing in your system, this is a sign that unwanted light is entering the tank. Every two or three years, remove the build-up of sludge at the bottom of the tank using a wet-and-dry vacuum or by hiring a contractor with the appropriate equipment. An alternative is to fit an internal tank vacuum that works by siphoning sludge when the tank is overflowing during a significant rainfall event.

Sustainable technologies involving water capture and storage are constantly improving, so do your own research to find the latest information. There is a lot of free, government-supported information available on the internet. Where appropriate and necessary, it is worth engaging professional help.

DAM AND POND WATER

For those gardeners fortunate enough to live on acreage, a dam represents an incredibly cost-effective way to store water for when there are not enough rainy days. Smaller gardens can also collect stormwater in ponds that can double as a water feature as well as storage. While it is much more difficult to control the quality of water in dams and ponds because they are open to the elements, they are nevertheless excellent options for harvesting and storing large volumes of water, and can also create environmentally friendly landscape features that will service wildlife and farm animals alike. In addition, the water in dams and ponds can usually be used by firefighters during bushfires.

The first thing to consider is the legal requirements concerning ponds and dams.

Left: All types of water-storage tanks should be inspected at regular intervals to prevent fouling of the water.

Opposite: A newly constructed dam at Angus's local community garden stores run-off from the site to provide irrigation water via a solar-powered pump for a small nursery, a vegie garden and various landscape plantings during the dry summers on the Tasmanian east coast.

Water resources are managed by each state government, so check the regulations governing how much water you can legally harvest from your property (you do have certain rights with regard to the volume of water versus the area of land you hold). There may be other considerations, such as the presence of endangered plant or animal species on your property. Safety fencing may be required to prevent accidental drowning, even around small ponds. Many local councils require a development application to be approved before any dam digging is undertaken, and this will take into account your impact on the water flow to neighbouring properties. Do your research at state and local government levels on both your entitlements to harvest water as well as your legal obligations.

Building and maintaining a dam

Siting your dam is a critical decision. Spring-fed dams are highly desirable if you can locate a spot on your property where subsurface water finds its way to the soil surface. This means that your dam will refill from subsurface water all year round, as well as collecting surface water run-off. How do you find a spring? Look for wet spots on your land, particularly in the days and weeks after a significant rainfall event has occurred. If you are still seeing puddles and wet spots when the surrounding ground has dried out, then they are likely to be the result of an underground spring.

The next best option – if it is both legal and possible – is to use a site that appears to catch a significant flow of surface run-off from a nearby watercourse, such as a creek bed that is normally

Dams can be environmentally friendly features that service wildlife and farm animals alike.

dry. It is particularly important to consult local and state authorities before going ahead with dams on or close to any sort of natural watercourse, in case it negatively affects the nearby environment.

It is well worth seeking expert advice while in the planning stage of your dam, as there are significant elements that go into creating a successful dam for long-term water storage. Soil type and geology are critical. Sandy or loamy (a mixture of sand, silt and clay) soils are naturally porous and will need modification if they are to hold water for any length of time. Using a waterproof membrane or a clay layer to line the dam will help with water retention.

Maintaining the dam is crucial for its long-term sustainability. Stock such as cattle can

do a lot of damage, which can cause leaks in dam walls. Regular inspection of your dam is essential so that problems can be arrested early, before the damage becomes irreversible.

Clay particles are fine enough to remain suspended in dam water over long periods of time, creating muddy and discoloured water that can clog irrigation systems. In this case, you can clear the muddiness by adding calcium-rich material such as gypsum to the water. This causes the clay particles to stick together and form aggregations that drop to the bottom of the dam. Bags of gypsum are cheap and readily available from hardware stores, or you can use aluminium sulphate. We recommend trying gypsum first, as this is successful in most situations and is cost-effective.

Left: Capillary irrigation through a 'do it yourself' wicking bed (see page 82) is a perfect way to optimise the use of precious water supplies.

BORE WATER

It is hard to overstate the importance of the water resource that is stored under the Earth's surface in aquifers, sometimes hundreds of metres deep. The quantity and quality of water available from underground aquifers varies widely according to the local geology and the water quality that is recharging the particular aquifer. As it is an expensive exercise to drill and establish a bore – and you are not guaranteed to strike a suitable water supply – it is advisable to do plenty of research before making this decision.

The water in many bores has a high level of dissolved salts, and it may also have a high or low pH; both factors can make it problematic to use that bore water on your garden. There are, of course, ways of treating the bore water if that is your only reliable water option (which

is often the case in the drier parts of Australia). For instance, iron minerals are sometimes successfully removed by spraying the water into the air, which causes the minerals to oxidise and fall to the bottom of the collection tank (which will then need regular cleaning). Technologies such as desalination are also available if the cost–benefit equation justifies it; careful research is needed before committing precious capital to this enterprise. If a source of good-quality water is available, then you can mix this water with the lesser-quality bore water to dilute the excess salts.

Groundwater-resource management is a state-government responsibility, so it is important to check on the rules and regulations surrounding groundwater extraction; however, in general, a property owner has the right to extract groundwater for household use. Large-scale extraction for agriculture or horticulture is an entirely different matter. Therefore, it is essential to establish your legal entitlements before spending tens of thousands of dollars on sinking a bore. The technical aspects of sinking a bore are best left to professional contractors. They will also have good local knowledge of the aquifers in your area, and this makes them a logical starting point for your research.

RECYCLED WATER

One of the tragic wastes of potable water is its use for purposes that do not require drinking-quality water. A better option is to make use of recycled water from various sources for suitable applications, such as flushing toilets or providing supplementary water for ornamental garden beds. There are two categories of household wastewater that can be recycled:

1 **Blackwater** comes from toilets, and it generally carries faecal contamination, so it has the potential to make us sick. It needs to be treated before it can be re-used in any way.

2 **Greywater** comes from baths, sinks and washing machines, and it will have varying levels of contamination that affect how it can be used.

Blackwater goes into either a municipal sewerage system where it is treated in bulk, or an on-site system such as a **septic tank** that gradually purifies the water through the action of beneficial microbes that are naturally present. If your septic system has an unpleasant odour, it may need to be pumped out because the system is full and could potentially overflow, or it may have a build-up of the wrong kinds of microbes. There are microbe cultures (such as the Australian product Actizyme) that can be flushed down your toilet to help tip the balance in favour of beneficial microbes.

Greywater is an inherently variable liquid because of its diverse origins, but the thing to stress is that we have a great deal of control over what gets added to our water when we wash our clothes, dishes and bodies. Indeed, some of the water that is designated as 'grey' has nothing whatsoever added to it (for instance, think of all the clean water that goes down the drain while you are waiting for the hot water to flow from your tap). Called 'fresh greywater', it can be collected and used without treatment, and this can be as simple as putting a bucket under the shower while you wait for the water to heat up. Angus uses a jug in the kitchen to collect such water, which then goes on his indoor pot plants – it's really a no-brainer.

What we might call 'soapy' greywater typically contains various cleaning agents, such as soaps, detergents and shampoos. It can also contain faecal matter, especially if you are washing dirty cloth nappies. This type of greywater (sometimes known as 'dark greywater') may contain a significant amount of harmful bacteria and should be sterilised using a water-treatment system before it is used on the garden. The various substances in soapy greywater can affect beneficial soil life, so use this water with care. It also pays to research the products you are using in your bathroom and laundry, as there is considerable variability in the ingredients. We'll have more about that subject later.

GOLDEN RULES OF GREYWATER

Avoid re-using greywater anywhere that may risk the health of people or pets. For example, do not use greywater on the vegetable garden. It may contain chemicals that are harmful to plant growth or soil health, such as detergents that contain a lot of sodium (salt).

Never store untreated greywater for more than 24 hours, as disease-causing microbes (that may be present in negligible amounts in newly generated greywater) can multiply to much higher (and therefore more dangerous) numbers over time.

TREAT YOUR GREYWATER RIGHT

If you create a large amount of greywater and/or you are in a sensitive environmental area such as a water catchment, your only option may be to install a water-treatment plant that will produce an abundance of purified greywater that can be used on ornamental gardens. Head to your local council to find out what the legal requirements are for your property. Installation of a greywater-treatment plant is definitely a job for a professional, so seek out expert advice and help when you are ready to go.

Far left: Greywater can be used on fruit and nut trees if it is delivered under the soil surface.

Left: Scorched leaf margins are an early warning sign of a build-up of toxic levels of soil salinity.

Using greywater

A simple way to collect greywater is to use buckets. You can also install a diversion device in your plumbing system that enables you to choose whether the soapy water (especially the dirtier water from your washing machine) goes to your sewerage pipes or to a small tank connected to a garden-irrigation system. This allows you to use the cleanest water after diverting any that is more heavily contaminated to the public sewerage system, where it will be safely treated.

The bucket method is both the easiest and cheapest, and it's a great way to save fresh water from washing and cooking vegetables, and while waiting for the shower to warm up. If you're also using buckets to collect soapy water, make sure to use a different bucket so you can keep the fresh and soapy water separate.

There are a few things to look out for when using soapy greywater in the garden. Don't put it on top of the soil – channel it underground through pipes or other means to reduce the risk of children and pets being exposed to harmful microbes. Use fresh greywater on vegetable and herb gardens, and use soapy greywater on lawns, ornamental plants, trees and shrubs. Interestingly, soapy water can be used on fruit and nut trees if it is delivered under the soil surface so that it doesn't come into contact with the edible parts of the plant.

The potential impacts of soapy greywater on soil salinity, pH and phosphorus levels in particular are the critical aspects for soil and plant health. Most washing products contain salts (including phosphorus) that, by design, create alkaline conditions that dissolve stains and get rid of dirt; however, these substances will also interact with your soil and its biology. This can cause symptoms such as discoloured leaf growth, especially the yellowing of new foliage. A build-up of salinity from the various components of cleaning products (such as sodium) causes scorching of leaf margins and growing tips, and a collapse in soil structure (particularly in clayey soils). This can be solved

The bucket method is a great way to save fresh water from washing and cooking vegetables, and while waiting for the shower to warm up.

PLANTS THAT COPE WELL WITH GREYWATER

These alkaline-loving plants are relatively tolerant of the effects of soapy greywater.

* bracelet honey myrtle (*Melaleuca armillaris*)
* coastal rosemary (*Westringia fruticosa*)
* hibiscus
* hop goodenia (*Goodenia ovata*)
* olive (*Olea europaea*)
* pigface (*Carpobrotus rossii*)
* pomegranate (*Punica granatum*)
* rosemary (*Rosmarinus officinalis*)
* spotted gum (*Corymbia maculata*)
* swamp oak (*Casuarina glauca*)
* weeping bottlebrush (*Callistemon viminalis*)
* yuccas

Hibiscus

Hop goodenia (*Goodenia ovata*)

Pigface (*Carpobrotus rossii*)

Waratah

Camellia

Grevillea 'Flamingo'

PLANTS THAT ARE SENSITIVE TO GREYWATER

These acid-loving plants are relatively intolerant of the effects of soapy greywater.

* banksias
* blueberries
* camellias
* citrus
* ferns
* geebungs (*Persoonia* species)
* grevilleas
* hakeas
* mountain devil (*Lambertia formosa*)
* rainforest plants, including many common indoor plants
* rhododendrons
* waratahs (*Telopea* species and cultivars)

Left: Coastal habitats are an excellent place to discover different species that thrive in salty conditions, such as manuka (*Leptospermum scoparium*).

by leaching your soil with copious quantities of fresh water (heavy rain will also do the job for you). Sandy soils are much more forgiving when it comes to soapy greywater because of their chemically inert nature.

Spreading your use of soapy greywater across as big an area of your garden as possible will help to dilute any potential problems. Don't allow greywater to pool on the surface (particularly where children or pets may play), or use it within a metre of your boundary, in-ground pool or in-ground potable water tank. Only use greywater when your soil needs watering to avoid it pooling or running off.

To further safeguard good soil health, regularly add plenty of organic matter such as compost or worm castings to areas where plants are showing symptoms of nutrient problems, as this will improve the soil structure as well as the pH and nutrient balance of the soil. Biochar is another important soil additive, as it absorbs and neutralises any harmful effects of soapy greywater. Another option to treat alkaline soil is to add iron sulphate or

wettable sulphur; test your soil pH to work out how much you need to add.

Of course, the best solution is to choose products designed to minimise any detrimental impact on your garden. Various independent websites provide information about this subject, including that of consumer advocacy group Choice. Look for the NP logo on packaging, as this indicates little to no phosphorus in the product. This minimises the chances of excess phosphorus ending up in waterways, where it can cause toxic algal blooms.

Some plants are more sensitive than others to greywater. Those that tolerate salty soils (such as seaside plants) and/or prefer alkaline soils adapt better to greywater use, while acid-loving plants (such as camellias and azaleas) will be much less tolerant. Phosphorus-sensitive native plants – such as those from the banksia family (Proteaceae) – may struggle to tolerate greywater, but there are plenty of natives that can cope, such as those from the eucalyptus family (Myrtaceae). For plants that are particularly sensitive and for your vegetable garden, you can use fresh greywater.

3

THE SCIENCE OF IRRIGATION

At first glance, watering your plants is a simple exercise and great therapy after a hard week at work. We apply water and fill up the pore spaces in the soil so the plants have a full reservoir from which to draw moisture. But how much water is enough, and how do we know that we are getting the water to where it is most needed?

In a lot of ways, watering plants can be a bit hit and miss if we don't have access to the science of irrigating plants. In this chapter, we take a look at that science to see how it can be applied to your individual situation.

The science of watering is well established, as the success or failure of irrigation can make or break agricultural and horticultural enterprises, so there is a great deal of technology available to monitor this all-important aspect of farming. This technology is usually beyond the reach of the home gardener; however, if we can understand the principles involved in keeping plants and their growing media supplied with water, then the average gardener can go a long way to being as efficient as possible with water usage while still getting your plants to achieve your gardening goals.

Some species can be trained to grow virtually without the need for irrigation, and you could choose from these to grow a garden of drought-tolerant Australian native plants (see pages 166–219) or cacti from various deserts around the world. However, your vegetable garden needs a different approach, as vegetables require a constant moisture supply to reach their full potential. Solutions such as wicking beds can offer a wonderful compromise – allowing you to grow vegetables but also use water as efficiently as possible.

So why not just water until we are absolutely sure our soil or growing mix is fully saturated? Although it is important to avoid water stress in our plants, it is also vital to avoid overwatering,

which not only wastes our precious water supply, but also potentially leaches away nutrients that have become dissolved in that soil water. The leaching of nutrients can cause problems in our waterways, such as toxic algal blooms, and wastes all the money you have spent on fertilisers because they never get the chance to be taken up by your plants as intended.

How do we make sure that we supply just enough water for our plants to do what we want them to do? Measuring the water content of our soil sounds like a logical way to establish when and how much water to give our plants. Unfortunately, it is not quite that simple – the total water content does not tell us about how **available** that water is to plant roots, as the type of soil we are working with has a huge impact on how easy or difficult it is for our plants to extract that water. Plants will find it much more difficult to extract water from a soil dominated by clay, with its fine particles, than a sandy soil with coarse particles.

Overwatering not only wastes our precious water supply, but also potentially leaches away nutrients that have become dissolved in the soil water.

A simple way to ensure that a plant receives just the right amount of water is to do it by hand, such as with a watering-can.

Opposite (clockwise from top left): A garden based on drought-tolerant plants – such as cacti and agaves – will naturally need less irrigation than other gardens; wicking beds (see pages 79–95) are ideal for thirsty plants such as vegies; roundleaf pigface (*Disphyma crassifolium*) is a native succulent that makes an excellent water-smart garden plant.

Far left and left: The Chameleon Card System utilises sensors that are buried in the soil and linked to monitors to give an instantaneous reading of moisture levels and to transmit data via the internet.

When it comes to watering your plants, the most useful thing you can do is measure the soil's moisture potential.

MOISTURE POTENTIAL VERSUS WATER CONTENT

When it comes to watering your plants, as well as building your soil's capacity for storing water (see Chapter 4), the most useful thing you can do is measure the soil's **moisture potential** – in other words, the **tenacity** with which the soil holds on to water, and the force or energy that plant roots need to exert to extract that water. Interestingly, while clay is very good at storing moisture, it is also very good at holding on to that water against the force of gravity and against the suction force exerted by plant roots. This is obviously a rather technical subject, but fortunately a principal research scientist at the CSIRO, Dr Richard Stirzaker, has come up with an easy way to work out a soil's moisture potential, and home gardeners can use the system.

The CSIRO Chameleon Card System

This is a very clever and incredibly simple method of calculating your soil's moisture potential at any particular moment in time. The Chameleon Card System was originally developed for small-scale farmers who were looking to maximise their water efficiency. It consists of sensors that are buried at different depths in the soil, with wires reaching to the surface that transmit an electrical impulse. When an electronic card is temporarily hooked up to the wires, it provides a reading that reveals the moisture potential of the soil. The clever part of the system is that, rather than the reading being a complicated set of numbers, it registers the information as colours: green for wet soil, blue for moist soil (which corresponds to your soil being at field capacity – the sweet spot for your garden plants) and red for dry soil (which corresponds to permanent wilting point for your plants – somewhere you definitely do not want your soil to be).

The system can be used to work out when to irrigate and – equally importantly – for how long to irrigate to get the water down as far as we want it to go in the soil profile. This will enable us to encourage plant roots to grow as deeply as possible to find the additional moisture that is stored in the subsoil. This is one of the keys to water-efficient gardening. If we can keep our growing medium in the 'blue zone' (see the photo on page 57), then we can keep the plants in the 'grow zone', meaning greater productivity for less water input. This is absolutely critical if your water supply is finite, such as from a rainwater tank. We also need to ensure that the other factors in plant growth – such as temperature and nutrient quantities – are at levels that enable the plants to take advantage of the water you are giving them.

The Chameleon Card sensors can be used in isolation with a card reader that will give an instantaneous reading at any time it is required. This can be used to learn how the soil or potting mix is behaving with respect to water usage, while giving precise information on when you need to water your plants. Alternatively, linking the system to a smartphone allows the data to be relayed to a website maintained by the CSIRO, and enables the user to log on and look at the accumulated data for their site. This data can be used to ascertain patterns throughout months, seasons and years, enabling very precise management of irrigation.

The Chameleon Card System can be a very useful tool for the home gardener, especially if you rely on a rainwater tank to irrigate. It can be moved around the garden to locate any differences in ambient moisture levels. Subsurface water movement can result in springs, which are semi-permanent moist spots in the garden.

TRAINING TREES

We have been using the Chameleon Card System at our tree plantation in Tasmania, with the objective of training the root systems down as far as possible into the subsoil. Three sensors are constantly collecting data on the moisture levels at depths of 20, 40 and 60 centimetres, so we can know when the water levels are depleting at each depth during a dry spell. Using this data, we can ensure that there is enough moisture at the lower depths to encourage the tree roots to reach down to those levels. The trees then become more self-sufficient and able to seek out any moisture that becomes available in the soil profile.

Pot plants usually need to be watered more frequently than plants growing in the ground.

WATERING FAQ

Over the years, we have found that gardeners tend to ask the same questions about the subject of watering their plants. Here are our answers to a variety of common irrigation queries – hopefully you will find them informative.

How often should I water my plants?

The water requirements for any given plant are constantly changing, and they will vary greatly on a seasonal basis. Many, but not all, plants are dormant in winter, with virtually zero irrigation needed. Also, consider a deciduous species that loses all of its leaves in winter: it needs almost no water while it is leafless, which incidentally is a great time to transplant it if necessary. A plant will obviously require much more water on hot, windy days and when it is actively growing and flowering.

The depth of the plant's root system will also affect its ability to extract moisture. Plants can extend their root system to seek out moisture in the subsoil, and we can encourage this through deep watering once a week; if this is successful, the plant will need watering less often. Pot plants usually need to be watered more frequently, as the amount of water that can be stored in the limited volume of potting mix is finite compared with the much greater volume of water that can be found in a garden's subsoil, where plant roots have the freedom to seek out moisture.

How much water should I use on my plants?

This is one of those 'How long is a piece of string?' questions. And the answer, of course, is that it depends on several factors. These include:

* the texture of your soil (more water is stored in a clayey soil than a sandy soil)
* the type of plant (deep-rooted woody plants versus shallow-rooted annuals)
* how deep the roots are at that particular moment in time
* the annual growth cycle of the plant (most species have seasonal growth spurts, and these vary from species to species)
* the time of year (plants will need more water in summer than in other seasons).

If you do not have a system like the Chameleon Card System mentioned earlier in this chapter, then you can gauge how much water you need to apply by taking an open can and digging it into your soil so the top is level with the soil surface. Check the can occasionally as you water; when it has 25–50 millimetres of water in the bottom of it, dig a hole in the soil to see how far the water has penetrated. If it has reached as far down as you need it to, then repeat the process until you work out how much water needs to be applied to different areas of your garden. As a general rule of thumb for most gardens, apply 25–50 millimetres of water each week from the beginning of spring to the end of summer, and much less in winter (depending on the plant species you are growing).

What is the best time of day to water?

It is best to water at either the beginning or the end of the day. The hottest part of the day is around midday, and a significant amount of water will be lost to evaporation if you water your plants at this time. It is also best to avoid watering when it is windy, as this will increase evaporation, especially if you are using sprinklers. However, if your plants are wilting at any time of the day, then that is by far the best time to water them to minimise your plants' stress.

What if the water won't soak into the soil?

Hydrophobic soils are relatively common in gardens, and occur when soils (and even potting mixes) actually repel water. You may see sphere-like water droplets forming on the surface; this is often referred to as 'beading' because of the water beads that form. This can become a big problem when you are on sloping ground, as water running off your soil is likely to cause erosion. If you have a hydrophobic soil that has any amount of clay in it, water can also be channelled through cracks, and the chunks of soil on either side of the cracks may not get watered properly. Sandy soils are also often hydrophobic. Potting mixes that are hydrophobic are extremely difficult to wet evenly, resulting in uneven and stunted plant growth.

It is always a great hands-on exercise to dig under the soil or potting mix surface to check the penetration and evenness of watering, as water-repelling media can be totally dry in parts even after a considerable amount of water has been applied to the surface. There are several remedies for hydrophobic soils and potting mixes:

* **Apply soil-wetting agents** – there are a number of products available, such as Wettasoil. These are easily made up in a watering-can and watered over the affected soil as required. After their use, water is attracted to the soil rather than being repelled. SaturAid is another product that supplies a wetting agent, but in this case it comprises granules that can be dug through soil or potting mix.

* **Use mulches** – water repellence only becomes evident when a susceptible soil dries out completely. Using mulch will conserve moisture and will greatly reduce the possibility of the soil drying out. Organic mulches – such as pine bark or eucalypt chips – are most effective, as they tend to hold moisture on top of the soil while it gradually soaks in rather than allowing the water to run off and cause erosion.

* **Dig in new material** – this can be non-hydrophobic soil, well-rotted manure or compost.

* **Create a moat** – a channel around any new plant will retain the water around the base of the plant, as even a hydrophobic soil will eventually let some water in.

* **Submerge the plant** – for potted plants that have become very hard to re-wet, you need to submerge the whole pot in a bucket of fresh water. You will be amazed at the number of air bubbles that escape as they are replaced in the soil by water from the bucket. It is also advisable to add a liquid seaweed preparation to the water, as this can help to alleviate the problem.

WATER MOVEMENT

One of the most important concepts to understand when it comes to watering plants is the **wetting front** – the way that water moves in soil or potting mix. It is always an interesting exercise to water your plant and then dig a hole nearby or knock it out of its pot to see how far down your irrigation effort has taken the water. We are still surprised on occasions to find that what we thought was a thorough watering has only penetrated just below the surface.

It is really handy to monitor the wetting front of the irrigation process we are carrying out. In the home garden, this can be done simply by trial and error (especially for potted plants, which we can remove from the pot). Digging a hole so that you expose a profile of your soil allows you to monitor the movement of an in-ground wetting front. This is vital in tracking the supply of not only water to the plant roots, but also nutrients to the plant. All of the nutrients that are supplied to the plant via the soil – such as phosphorus, potassium, iron and many others – have to first be dissolved in soil water before any plant can take them up.

Opposite (clockwise from top left): A liquid wetting agent is being sprayed onto hydrophobic soil; a mulch layer should be no thicker than 5 centimetres; loosen the soil in the bottom and at the sides of planting holes to make it easier for new roots to penetrate; dunk your plants in water, pot and all, before planting to give them the best moisture level for rapid establishment.

One of the most important concepts to understand when it comes to watering plants is the wetting front – the way the water moves in soil or potting mix.

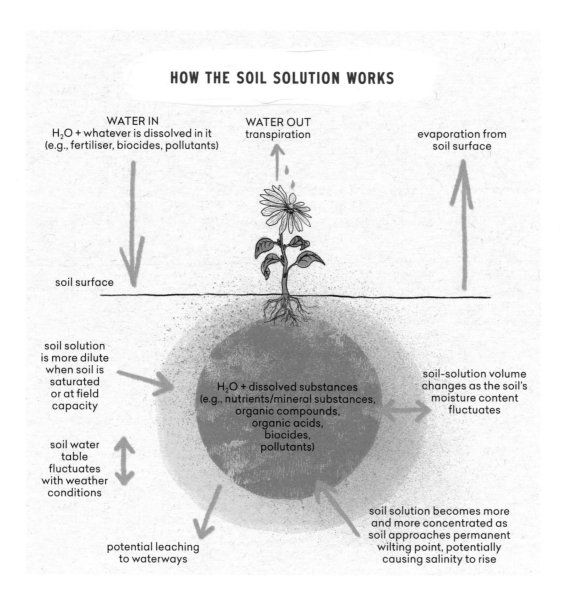

HOW THE SOIL SOLUTION WORKS

WATER IN
H_2O + whatever is dissolved in it
(e.g., fertiliser, biocides, pollutants)

WATER OUT
transpiration

evaporation from
soil surface

soil surface

soil solution
is more dilute
when soil is
saturated
or at field
capacity

H_2O + dissolved substances
(e.g., nutrients/mineral substances,
organic compounds,
organic acids,
biocides,
pollutants)

soil-solution volume
changes as the soil's
moisture content
fluctuates

soil water
table
fluctuates
with weather
conditions

potential leaching
to waterways

soil solution becomes more
and more concentrated as
soil approaches permanent
wilting point, potentially
causing salinity to rise

The soil solution

Depending on the source of your water, it is pretty much pure H_2O when it first enters the soil. However, as soon as it soaks into the soil, all sorts of different substances dissolve in it, so that **soil water then becomes a soil solution**. In particular, the various minerals – such as nitrates, phosphates and sulphates that supply plants with the essential elements for growth – are perhaps the most important to get a handle on. Soil water can also carry other water-soluble chemicals, such as pesticides, weedicides or perhaps heavy metals (such as lead from old paint residue). Whatever is dissolved in the soil

solution moves with the wetting front, sometimes displacing the substances that were already in the soil prior to the thorough watering.

The soil solution is a dynamic thing that changes constantly as the soil's moisture content fluctuates. For instance, during a dry spell, some of the water in the soil solution will evaporate. This can lead to a concentration of dissolved salts in the remaining solution, which can create a level of soil salinity that is harmful to your plants. The soil solution can be easily extracted from the soil so we can measure vital parameters for plant growth, such as pH and salinity, as well as the presence of any toxic substances.

Left: If you need to get nutrients into your plants quickly, then liquid feeding them is the answer.

Liquid feeding is the fastest and most effective way to get nutrients to your precious plants. Understanding how the application of a liquid feed plays out in the soil will help you to maximise the benefits while minimising any loss of nutrients. When we introduce any liquid fertiliser to our soil, we will make big changes to the composition of the soil solution, as the nutrients mix with whatever was there originally. As this newly altered soil solution fills up the pore spaces in the soil, it creates a wetting front that moves down through the soil and carries whatever is dissolved in the solution down with it. It tends to displace and replace the dissolved salts that were there before the liquid fertiliser was applied. This has all sorts of important consequences, especially if your soil has an existing problem with salinity, because any fertiliser adds salts to whatever is already there.

RESTRICTIONS ON WATERING

Drought conditions can overtake us at any time in Australia, often resulting in local authorities imposing restrictions on when and how we can water our gardens. If you are in any doubt about this issue, it is best to check with your local council or water authority. This is the time when having your own rainwater tanks can really provide your garden with an escape clause. Rationing that water out by using the most water-efficient growing systems and techniques, especially in the fruit and vegetable garden, is vitally important.

The most popular irrigation
system is hand-watering.
A moat around the plant
will channel this water to
where it's needed, and is
especially useful if your
soil is hydrophobic.

IRRIGATION SYSTEMS

There are many different options when it comes to delivering water to a growing plant. It can be as simple as using a watering-can, bucket or garden hose (which would be a last resort in dire situations such as very dry spells) to water in new plantings, or it can be as complicated as installing an elaborate automated irrigation system controlled remotely from your smartphone.

Some aspects of irrigation installation can be a do-it-yourself enterprise, but there are other aspects that are best left to the professionals, particularly where there are tricky government regulations involved, such as the prevention of backflow into town water supplies. Suppliers and distributors of irrigation equipment such as hardware stores and garden centres are excellent sources of advice and information about what you can attempt versus what a professional should do. The initial design of any reasonably complex irrigation system will generally benefit greatly from the input of an irrigation professional.

Choosing the most appropriate irrigation system for your situation will depend on a number of factors, including:

* **environmental conditions** – knowing the type of soil you have in your garden is critical. For sandy soils, water storage is low but infiltration rate is high, making drip irrigation an ideal method because it delivers smaller quantities of water more often. Soils with greater clay content tend to have opposite characteristics to sandy soils, meaning that a wider range of irrigation systems can do the job efficiently. Sloping sites lend themselves more to sprinkler and drip irrigation.

* **water availability** – if water is scarce, then techniques such as wicking beds that utilise subsurface irrigation are much more efficient. These systems eliminate any evaporation from the soil surface.

* **water quality** – if the water (such as that from a dam) has a lot of sediment in it, then sprinklers and drippers tend to get

IRRIGATION VERSUS DRYLAND GROWING SYSTEMS

An important decision when planning your garden is whether it will be given extra water when needed, or if it will be treated as a dryland situation – to use an agricultural term – where the plants must rely solely on natural water sources such as rainfall. In dryland situations, a good rainfall season allows the plants to reach their full growing potential, but a poor rainfall season means that plants may struggle to produce any growth or crops at all. If you choose to go this way, it is helpful to select plant species such as succulents and Australian plants from low-rainfall areas, as these can survive long dry periods without suffering unduly. In the end, the question of whether to irrigate or not often comes down to whether you have a suitable and economically viable source of irrigation water, and whether you want to go to the trouble and expense of installing an irrigation system.

clogged. Other irrigation methods may be much more efficient in the long term.

* **climate** – very windy climates make sprinkler systems difficult to operate. Drip or capillary irrigation is a much more efficient way to go.

Let's look at the various options available, proceeding roughly from the least expensive to the most expensive irrigation systems. We will note the pros and cons of each for the home gardener.

Surface irrigation

This is where gravity is used to distribute water around the surface of the area to be irrigated. In agricultural systems, the land is sculpted to channel water across a field so that every plant is watered evenly, an important consideration when vast areas are planted with one particular crop species.

In a home garden, where we are growing lots of different plants with varying moisture requirements, we can use mounds and swales to keep rainwater on-site and to channel that stormwater to where it is most needed. This means that we can give each species or variety exactly the environmental conditions it needs to thrive.

Hand-watering around the base of a plant is a time-honoured method of delivering surface irrigation, but it is labour intensive. When we hand-water, we often have a tendency to not apply enough water, as it takes longer than we imagine for surface irrigation to reach right down to the bottom of the root zone.

Drip (trickle) irrigation

Small emitters that release droplets of water at regular intervals are the basis of drip irrigation. It is one of the most water-efficient irrigation methods available, as the water enters the soil very quickly, reducing evaporation losses to virtually zero. Another huge advantage is that water can be delivered precisely to the target plants, which means that a lot less water is used compared with surface or sprinkler irrigation, and we are also not applying water to soil that will be potentially growing weeds. It is also an efficient way to deliver liquid fertiliser to your plants.

Drip irrigation runs on relatively low pressure, meaning that there is less risk of pipes blowing their seals and fewer powerful pumps are required – if it is designed appropriately, the system can be run entirely by using gravity. Drip systems can be easily automated with timers and valves to dramatically reduce the amount of labour required. The disadvantages of drip systems are the relative expense of installing the required infrastructure, and the tendency of the emitters

Above left:
Hand-watering plants with a hose is a time-consuming but relaxing pastime.

Above right:
This drip (trickle) irrigation system has the drippers enclosed inside the pipe and is an efficient way to water plants.

Left: Adjustable drip emitters can be installed using small-diameter 'spaghetti' tubing to allow for garden plants that are irregularly spaced.

to clog up if there are any large particulate contaminants in your irrigation water.

There is a great variety of technology available when it comes to drip irrigation, and some important choices need to be made when designing and installing a drip system. For instance, the emitters can be placed inside the pipe at predetermined intervals, which is excellent for vegetable crops that are planted in even rows. Alternatively, emitters can be installed externally on the pipe once the system has been put in place, which suits an ornamental garden where plants are spaced irregularly. Various emitters are available depending on how many litres per hour are required and the type of flow that is desired, such as drip versus mist versus larger droplets.

If you are willing to go to the expense of installing any sort of extensive drip irrigation system, then we strongly recommend using an expert to design and set up the system, as there are various pitfalls that can cause significant problems over time. This is especially true if you are on a sloping site, where the force of gravity adds extra pressure to the lowest emitters. You will need pressure-compensating emitters to ensure that every emitter delivers the same volume of water. Correct technology ensures that we can compensate for the extra pressure through clever design.

Some simple systems can be more of a do-it-yourself project, such as the so-called 'leaky pipe' that is attached to your garden tap and weeps water along its entire length. Recycled plastic (PET) drink bottles can be transformed into irrigation reservoirs that are particularly good for larger plants such as trees and shrubs. You fill the clean bottle with water and then bury it upside down (without its lid) in the soil; the water gradually seeps into the soil over time. Or you cut out the bottom of the bottle and bury it with the uncapped top poking out of the soil; you simply refill the bottle on a regular basis whenever you want to water your plant.

Another handy do-it-yourself option is to use agricultural subsurface drainage pipes (also known as ag-pipes) with perforated slots that

Left: To ensure that water reaches the deepest roots, install a vertical ag-pipe in the ground and fill it with water periodically.

Opposite: Portable sprinklers deliver relatively large volumes of water in a short space of time, but they waste water through evaporation.

Spray irrigation wastes a significant amount of water thanks to evaporation.

allow water to enter or exit the pipe along its length. Bury a 300–500-millimetre length of ag-pipe vertically beside a tree or shrub, with the end of the pipe poking out of the ground. This creates a mini reservoir in the soil next to your plant that allows water to gradually move into the soil every time you fill up the ag-pipe.

Spray (sprinkler) irrigation

This is a system in which pressurised irrigation water is sprayed over the target plants like rainfall. It is an effective way of quickly delivering a lot of water to the garden. As it is generally affordable and simple to install, a spray system is particularly suitable for lawns, and the whole system can be readily mechanised and automated if necessary. However, on the downside, spray irrigation wastes a significant amount of water thanks to evaporation, particularly on hot and/or windy days. Wind can also dramatically reduce the effectiveness of spray systems if it blows the

water away from where it is designed to go. Sediments and other contaminants in your irrigation water can also easily block up a spray system.

When it comes to designing and installing a spray system, there is a huge range of options available, from portable garden sprinklers and fixed sprinklers that remain in place permanently to 'pop-up' sprinklers that sink down into the soil when not in use, allowing for easier mowing and maintenance of lawns and gardens. Another extremely useful variation is the micro sprinkler. A number of these can be plugged into a flexible pipe (in the same way that drippers are installed), and they can be used to water intermediate areas (such as the drip line of trees and shrubs) without losing too much water to evaporation. Once again, it is best to consult an irrigation professional on the best system for your situation, and also whether you need a professional to install the system or you can do it yourself.

SAY HELLO TO THE OLLA

An olla (pronounced oi-ya) is an ancient irrigation system that has been used around the world for thousands of years. It is an unglazed terracotta clay container filled with water that is buried in the ground with its neck protruding so it can be easily refilled. Because the container is unglazed, it is porous; water seeps out of the sides of the container and into the soil around the root zone of plants growing nearby. In effect, the plant roots can access as much or as little water as they need. An optional extra is a small float topped with a flag that rises and falls with the water level, allowing you to gauge when the olla needs to be refilled.

The beauty of this concept is that once the soil around the olla is moist, the water seepage stops until the soil dries out again. So, if a rainfall event soaks the soil, the water remains in the olla. Unlike sprinkler irrigation systems, ollas waste very little water by evaporation and drainage through the soil profile.

We road-tested a variety of ollas of different sizes supplied to us by an Australian company called Up on the Rooftop, which specialises in gardening gear for small spaces such as courtyards and balconies – perfect applications for the olla. The accompanying photos show the installation and functioning of an olla that gave excellent results in our trial with minimal water use. Another unexpected advantage was that, while refilling the olla with a garden hose, we had time to weed around the crops being supplied with water by the olla.

Anticlockwise from top left: Fill the olla with water; dig a hole adjacent to the plants to be irrigated, deep enough to bury the olla while leaving the neck exposed; place the olla in the hole; backfill the hole up to the neck of the olla, so it can be regularly refilled.

SMALL-SPACE WATER SOLUTIONS

For those living in small urban spaces and rental properties, container gardening is the best way to cultivate a range of plants. Growing in containers offers some significant advantages as well as some challenges. One of the great advantages is the ability to control aspects such as drainage, soil composition and light levels. However, in terms of moisture, plants in containers need to be watered more often than plants in the ground, because pot plants don't have access to any water beyond their containers. Generally, the larger the container, the less frequently it will need to be watered, because the soil in it can store more moisture than the soil in a smaller pot. Watering frequency will also vary depending on the water needs, density and maturity of the plants in the pot.

Emma's garden in the Sydney suburb of Clovelly is on a concrete slab and is mostly in containers, with a few garden beds as well. Here are a few of her favourite plants and ways to manage water in a container garden.

WaterUps square planter

This compact planter is around half a metre square (480 millimetres [D] x 480 millimetres [W] x 430 millimetres [H]). It is a wicking bed (see pages 79–95) that can be used to grow herbs and vegetables as well as small fruit trees.

Emma has planted hers out with a mixture of Australian native food plants, including a cultivar of native sandpaper fig (*Ficus opposita*) called 'Sandpaper Bird's Eye' that has delicious dark red figs. It has been in the planter for almost two years now and started to produce a great crop of figs at the end of last year. It does need a bit

> Plants in containers need to be watered more often than plants in the ground, because pot plants don't have access to any water beyond their containers.

Opposite: The WaterUps square planter has proved to be perfect for growing thirsty bush-food plants.

Far left: A small terracotta water spike is placed into the potting mix in a large pot.

Left: A full bottle of water is inserted into the spike so that the water will slowly seep into the potting mix.

of extra water to produce a good crop of fruits, so it's perfect for this wicking bed. The leaves have the texture of fine-grained sandpaper and can be used as such.

In addition to the sandpaper fig, Emma has filled the planter with other edible plants of different shapes and sizes to make the most of the space. There is a variety of midyim berry (*Austromyrtus* 'Copper Tops'), as well as warrigal greens (*Tetragonia tetragonioides*) and river mint (*Mentha australis*) as ground covers that spill over the edges of the container as they mature. Most of these plants are perennial or self-seeding, so they don't require much maintenance.

The water reservoir needs to be filled about once a week in the heat of summer, and less frequently in the cooler seasons and during periods of rainy weather.

Terracotta water spikes

Terracotta water spikes function in the same way as ollas (see pages 72–3), but the water is stored in a bottle or vessel above the soil and slowly seeps out through the spike as the plant roots take up moisture. These are great for medium to large containers, and especially for thirsty plants that seem to need more water than others. The spike only delivers water to the area immediately around it, so it's a buffer against the soil drying out completely rather than an alternative to watering. The container still needs to be watered thoroughly over the whole root zone, but the spikes are great for maintaining soil moisture in hot weather, for thirsty plants or when you are away on a trip.

Moisture meter

These simple gadgets are cheap, widely available and great for managing water use in potted plants. They're very useful for container gardening because it can be hard to tell how moist the soil is at the deeper levels of the pot, particularly in very large containers. Some containers can also develop drainage problems depending on the potting mix used and how long the plant has been in the pot, and the moisture meter can help to diagnose these issues, too. It can also show you whether the soil in a pot has become hydrophobic and can't take up

water properly. If the meter shows that the soil is consistently dry even after deep watering, the soil has become hydrophobic and will need some intervention.

Self-watering (wicking) pots

Self-watering (wicking) pots are designed to hold a reservoir of water beneath the plant's roots, providing additional water as the pot dries out. They are particularly useful for indoor plants, as the plant can take up extra water as it needs. They can also be used for outdoor plants; however, they function best when the water levels can be regulated, so these pots are primarily used for indoor or covered areas.

There are a number of designs available: some have a moisture gauge, while others feature different ways of managing water overflow. If you are using these pots outdoors, an overflow outlet is necessary just in case they fill up with rainwater. Some have an overflow outlet with a removable plug, so they can be used indoors or outside. Self-watering pots use a similar principle to wicking beds (see pages 79–95), but they are much smaller in scale.

Opposite (clockwise from top left): A perforated raised platform is placed in the base of the self-watering (wicking) pot to create the water reservoir; a plug is inserted into the overflow outlet (this can be removed at any time to drain the reservoir if necessary); potting mix is added to the pot and firmed down to ensure that water wicks efficiently from the reservoir to the mix above; an indoor plant – in this case, a peace lily (*Spathiphyllum* species) – is planted into the self-watering (wicking) pot.

Left: A moisture meter helps to ensure even watering at the lower depths of plant containers.

THE AIRGARDEN

An Australian-made innovation, the Airgarden is a compact, water-smart, vertical hydroponic system. Hydroponics involves growing plants without soil, with essential nutrients obtained from an aqueous mineral solution that is supplied to the roots. The Airgarden is a branch of hydroponics known as aeroponics, because the plant roots are suspended in mid-air and regularly showered with the nutrient solution to stop them drying out. The system consists of a tower with many evenly spaced cup-shaped holes into which plants started off in small net-like pots are inserted. The tower has a large reservoir at the base in which a submersible pump is placed; the pump is used to constantly send the nutrient solution up to the top of the tower so it can then cascade down the walls of the tower and splash over the plant roots. This results in almost perfect growing conditions and therefore very high growth rates.

Because the system is fully self-contained, with the root systems growing inside the tower and the nutrient solution being continually recirculated, there is very little evaporation of the solution. This means that the amount of water used is small compared to what would be needed to grow the same plants in the ground or as conventional pot plants. Furthermore, the nutrient solution is regularly monitored

to keep the pH and nutrients at optimum levels. This ensures that the plants have everything they need to reach their full potential, with impressive results.

We certainly achieved very high productivity levels with the Airgarden for a wide variety of edible and ornamental species. It would be most useful for gardeners and commercial urban farmers who have limited space, because the tower is a vertical garden (it is perfect for courtyards and balconies in particular). Early-adopter cafes and restaurants are already using the system to grow fast crops, such as leafy greens and herbs that don't grow too tall.

The Airgarden requires maintenance at least once a week, which consists of topping up the reservoir with water and two-part nutrient concentrate, and checking the pH. This is not an onerous task and can be done at the same time as reaping a bountiful harvest. We found that in the middle of summer, when growth rates were at their peak, the topping-up process needed to be done every few days, but this corresponded with peak production when the fresh produce was coming thick and fast.

Overall, we found the Airgarden to be a huge success as a water- and nutrient-efficient way to keep fresh produce on the table all year round, but you must be prepared to keep the maintenance up on a weekly basis for the best results. An interesting observation was that various Australian bush-food plants we trialled – such as warrigal greens (*Tetragonia tetragonioides*) and sea celery (*Apium prostratum*) – performed brilliantly, and grew just as fast and bountifully as exotic crops such as lettuce and parsley.

CAPILLARY (SUBSURFACE) WATERING

Water molecules are attracted to solid surfaces such as soil particles and can be held there against the force of gravity, enabling soil to store moisture after rainfall or irrigation. Plant roots seeking out moisture will apply suction pressure to extract the water molecules from the soil particles. Because moisture content in the soil is constantly changing, the competing forces of attraction for the water molecules in soil water will result in movement of that water from areas of higher concentration towards those of lower concentration – thus water can move up, down or sideways via capillary action as the soil dries out, often unevenly, through the whole soil profile. We can take advantage of this phenomenon to create a soil environment in which we can use capillary movement of water to irrigate our plants.

Many gardeners have unwittingly applied the technique of capillary watering to their pot plants when they have placed the pots in a saucer or some other container to catch the water that drains away through the pot's holes. If the water that overflows into the sauce or container is left in place, the potting mix will gradually reabsorb it as the mix dries out during the days after watering.

Compared to overhead watering, capillary watering is a more effective way to irrigate plants for three reasons:

1   **It keeps the foliage dry,** helping to protect the plants against fungal leaf diseases such as powdery mildew.

2   **Less water is used overall,** because there is zero wastage.

3   **Very little if any water reaches the soil surface,** thus eliminating the loss of water via evaporation.

Wicking beds

Another name for the capillary movement of water is **wicking**, referring to the way a cotton wick works in a kerosene lamp (the kerosene molecules are attracted to the dry fibres of the cotton wick, which enables the kerosene molecules to overcome the force of gravity and move upwards). Wicking beds take advantage of the capillary movement of water, and they are a water-efficient way of growing plants. They offer significant advantages when they are used to cultivate edible plants that have been bred to grow and crop very quickly, and need optimum growing conditions to reach their full growth potential. Plants in a wicking bed are able to access water whenever they need it; as long as the reservoir is never allowed to run dry, your crops should never be water-stressed. Nutrient loss through leaching of fertilisers from the system is greatly reduced, particularly if you are careful to stop refilling the reservoir as soon as water starts to overflow from it.

When it comes to the disadvantages of wicking beds, the biggest single problem in our experience is the potential transmission of plant diseases through the somewhat closed system of a wicking bed. In a more conventional growing system, water can drain away through either the soil profile or the drainage holes in a pot, potentially taking any pathogenic organisms (such as root rot) away from plant roots. However, in a wicking bed where water is retained within the system, any disease-causing organisms that find their way in are retained as well, and they have the potential to spread rapidly right through the system. In particular, there are a number of root-rot diseases caused by fungi that are sometimes called water moulds, because these pathogens thrive and spread very quickly in moist to wet conditions. Many gardeners will have heard of the fungus *Phytophthora cinnamomi*, which is causing massive dieback problems in the Australian bush, particularly in Western Australia.

The potential for diseases to cause problems within a wicking bed can be minimised by maintaining excellent hygiene, in the same way we use measures such as hand-washing to minimise the risk of being infected with human pathogens. Be extra careful when introducing new plants and soil/potting mix, and keep your tools as clean as possible between jobs in different parts of your garden. Remove any diseased plants as soon as possible to minimise transmission of the pathogen.

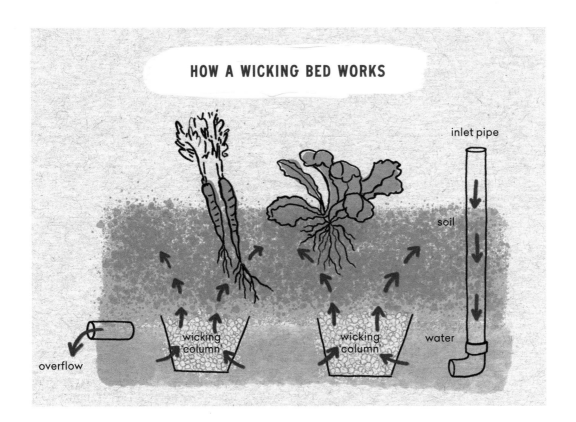

HOW A WICKING BED WORKS

inlet pipe

soil

water

wicking 'column'

wicking 'column'

overflow

There are two other disadvantages of wicking beds. Firstly, a wicking bed is more expensive to establish than an in-ground garden bed, and secondly, excess fertiliser use can see salt residues leaching down into the water reservoir and result in a build-up of salinity. The most common symptom of salinity in plants is scorching of the leaf margins. Flushing out the reservoir will help to alleviate the issue. In our experience, if you can afford the investment of a wicking bed then it is well worth using one, as its advantages far outweigh its disadvantages.

For a wicking bed to reach its full potential, there are various aspects that need to be optimised. The supply of nutrients requires careful consideration, as it tends to be more difficult to add fertiliser to a wicking bed than to in-ground beds. A good solution is to incorporate solid fertiliser in the potting mix and supplement it with the particular nutritional needs of the plants growing in the bed.

The reservoir at the base of the wicking bed stores the water, which then needs an efficient way to reach the growing medium above it.

Wicking 'columns' that extend from the bottom of the reservoir to the growing medium are essential, as they ensure that all of the stored water is actually available to be wicked up to the growing medium. A common mistake we have seen in wicking-bed construction is filling the reservoir with coarse gravel without incorporating wicking 'columns' within the gravel layer (for more information about this, see page 82). Wicking 'columns' should be filled with a porous material (such as perlite or biochar) and have holes at their base so that there is a mechanism for the water to wick up to the growing medium even when there is very little left in the reservoir.

The growing medium provides several things to enable optimal plant growth: support, water, nutrients and air. When selecting the growing medium for a wicking bed, it is important to make sure that it has the right balance of particle sizes to enable the water to wick up to the plant roots growing in it. The taller the bed, the harder it becomes to wick up water to shallow-rooted plants (such as newly planted seedlings), so you need a greater proportion of finer particles in taller beds. Choosing the right growing-media components is the key to optimising the performance of your wicking bed. Here are some of the best:

* **Perlite** is a volcanic mineral rock that is expanded by heating to form a lightweight material. As it is full of minute pore spaces, it is very good at both storing and wicking water. It is useful as a material for wicking water up from the reservoir to the growing medium above. It can also be a handy component of the growing medium, as it minimises the weight of the bed while helping water to wick up through the medium to the plant roots.

* **Coir fibre** is an organic material that is a by-product of coconut processing. Like perlite, it has excellent wicking properties as well as the ability to store water and nutrients.

* **Composted pine bark** is the by-product of milling pine trees for timber items. As it is composted, the pine bark does not rob nutrients from whatever potting mix it goes into. It comes in a variety of particle sizes that can be used to formulate potting mixes for different purposes.

* **Composted sawdust** is another by-product of the timber industry. It provides a relatively fine component for potting mixes that will facilitate the wicking process and help to store water and nutrients in the mix.

* **Expanded clay aggregates** provide a lightweight option for storing water and nutrients in a growing medium. As they are a mineral component, they do not break down and lose volume over time like organic components such as pine bark. A particle size of 2–10 millimetres is best, and the aggregates can make up 20–80 per cent of the growing-medium volume, depending on the plants being grown. Note that these aggregates are relatively expensive and are therefore best used where the extra cost can be justified.

Far left: A hose is used to fill a WaterUps wicking bed. See pages 88–9 for more information on the WaterUps system.

Left: Expanded clay aggregates are a porous and lightweight material that is perfect for wicking beds located on roofs.

DO-IT-YOURSELF WICKING BEDS

There are hundreds of videos online that show you how to build a wicking bed, but it is vital to understand the basic principles, as there is a lot of misinformation out there. One of the critical mistakes we often see is a wicking bed with no mechanism for the water to be wicked up from the bottom of the reservoir to the interface between the reservoir and the growing medium. Rather, the instructions often say that the reservoir should be filled with gravel. However, once the water level drops below the interface between the gravel and the growing medium, an air gap is formed that effectively makes it impossible for the water to wick upwards. A wicking 'column' is needed that goes from the bottom of the reservoir up to the interface, with this 'column' being filled with a porous material such as perlite or biochar. This ensures that the plants in the wicking bed can access the water in the reservoir.

If you want to save money, you can build a wicking bed from largely recycled materials. However, there are numerous ready-made systems that are simple to set up and very easy to use. You can buy stand-alone pots that utilise capillary watering; these come in many styles and colours, and are suitable for indoor and outdoor pot plants. Even regular pots with drainage holes can become mini wicking beds when placed in water. Simply match the pot size to a saucer or tray that holds enough water to properly irrigate the pot plant above. It works best with shorter pots, because the capillary rise of moisture in taller pots may not be sufficient to reach shallow-rooted plants.

A variation on this theme is to put a layer of gravel in the bottom of the saucer or tray to raise the humidity level around the foliage of the potted plant; this is particularly useful for indoor plants that originally come from humid rainforests. Most of the water in the saucer will be absorbed by the potting mix and 'wick' up to the roots; however, some of the water in the saucer will simply evaporate and raise the humidity in the immediate vicinity, increasing the moisture around the foliage as well as watering the plant. Ensure that the water level in the saucer is high enough to submerge the base of the pot, otherwise capillary watering of the pot will not occur.

Step 1

Step 3

Step 2

Step 4

Making a large wicking bed at home

All sorts of second-hand materials can be used to construct wicking-bed systems, as long as several basic principles are followed. The first is to create a framework to house the reservoir of water at the base, as well as the growing medium above; in this case, we used recycled hardwood offcuts that were fixed with screws. The second is to create a watertight reservoir at the base of the bed; here we used an offcut of vinyl flooring to create a smooth base for a food-grade plastic pond liner, which we purchased at the local hardware store. It is also extremely important to make sure that the base of the bed is as level as possible by using a long spirit level. Recycled 140-millimetre diameter plastic pots were used inside the liner, with most placed upside down to create a void for water storage. The third principle is to have wicking legs in the reservoir that are filled with a suitably porous material (such as perlite or biochar), which moves the water from the reservoir to the growing medium above. The fourth principle is to choose a growing medium with a balance of ingredients that will wick the water up to the plant roots growing in it. Most commercial potting mixes work well in this regard.

Step 1 Use an offcut of vinyl flooring or similar to create a smooth base at the bottom of the wicking bed. This will reduce the possibility of the pond liner being punctured during the life of the wicking bed.

Step 2 Cut a food-grade plastic pond liner to shape, and fit it to the inside of the wicking bed.

Step 3 Staple the pond liner to the inside of the wicking bed to keep it in place.

Step 4 Install an irrigation fitting to create an overflow outlet at the top of the reservoir. When the reservoir is completely filled, the excess water will flow from the outlet.

Steps continued >

Step 5 Fill the base of the wicking bed with upside-down, 140-millimetre diameter recycled plastic plant pots to create a void for the water. Keep some of the pots the right way up and fill them with a porous material (such as perlite) to enable the water to wick up to the growing medium.

Step 6 Cover the pots with a layer of geotextile fabric to prevent plant roots from growing down and clogging up the wicking legs. If you want to save money, you can use any porous material (such as a fabric offcut) rather than purchasing geotextile fabric.

Step 7 Fill the wicking bed with a suitable growing medium (such as a premium-grade potting mix).

Step 8 Insert the inlet pipe, a piece of irrigation poly pipe that is placed between the pots in the reservoir, and pack the growing medium around it. Water is added to the wicking bed via a garden hose in the inlet pipe.

Step 9 Plant the newly established wicking bed with your choice of seedlings (we planted broccoli here).

Step 10 When water flows from the overflow outlet, the reservoir is completely full and ready for action.

Step 5

Step 8

Step 6

Step 7

Step 9

Step 10

Making a small wicking bed at home

The principles of wicking beds can be applied at various scales. In this case, we have used a plastic crate and small recycled plant pots to create a mini wicking bed.

Step 1 Line a sturdy recycled plastic crate with a food-grade plastic pond liner, and install an overflow outlet on the side.

Step 2 Use a cable tie to fix the overflow outlet firmly in place.

Step 3 Fill the base of the wicking bed with upside-down, 50-millimetre diameter, recycled plastic tube pots to create the reservoir. Ensure some of them are the right way up and filled with perlite to create the wicking legs that move water up to the growing medium.

Step 4 Insert a short length of irrigation poly pipe between the pots so the reservoir can be filled.

Step 5 Cover the pots with a layer of geotextile fabric (or some other type of porous fabric) to prevent the plant roots from clogging up the wicking legs.

Step 6 Fill the wicking bed with a suitable growing medium (such as a premium-grade potting mix).

Step 7 Plant the wicking bed with your choice of seedlings (we planted an Australian native mint here).

Step 1

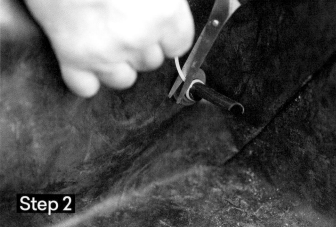

Step 2

Step 5

Step 3

Step 4

Step 6

Step 7

Commercial wicking-bed systems

WaterUps is an elegantly simple capillary-watering system from an innovative Australian company. It is modular and highly adaptable to different situations. The system revolves around a specially designed wicking 'tile' that is made from fully recycled but very durable food-grade plastic. The tile sits on four 'legs' that have slits in the bottom to allow water to wick up into the suitable material (such as perlite) that has been used to fill the legs. A layer of geotextile fabric on top of the tile stops roots from growing into the legs but is not essential to the functionality of the system. The individual tiles are 400 millimetres square by 130 millimetres high and are designed to sit at the bottom of a waterproof membrane.

Each tile has a hole where an inlet pipe is installed, into which a hose can be inserted to fill the reservoir that is formed underneath the tile. The provision of a small outlet at the top of the tile allows for an overflow pipe to be installed; this not only tells you when the reservoir below is full, but also ensures that you do not overfill the wicking bed. WaterUps has a number of ready-to-assemble above-ground wicking-bed kits available, ranging from a single-tile planter box to larger units constructed from Colorbond. Professional-grade shadecloth covers are also available, and they can be fitted over the beds to protect the plants from insect pests (such as aphids) and animal pests (such as possums). Our trials with these units gave us exceptional growth rates, while using only 20 per cent of the water needed for a conventional raised garden bed.

The WaterUps tiles can also be cut with an angle grinder or saw so you can create wicking beds in other watertight containers, such as old, round, corrugated-iron water tanks. The modular nature of the WaterUps system offers an easy way to create wicking beds that can be of almost

Above: Watering this rooftop wicking-bed garden is as simple as turning on a hose tap when the reservoir is nearly dry.

Far left: Emma grows a variety of crops in her Vegepod.

Left: The Vegebag is perfect for balconies and small gardens.

any size and shape, something we have not seen elsewhere. It's a very clever Australian invention!

Yet another inventive Australian company has come up with a couple of very useful mobile, low-input, low-maintenance growing systems that are particularly well suited for growing food crops (and other plants) in small spaces. The **Vegepod** is a relatively compact wicking bed that has the option of being mounted on a stand with wheels to allow it to be moved around the garden, balcony or courtyard. It also has a removable hood with a built-in sprinkler system that can be connected to a garden hose via a snap-on fitting. Or it can be watered by hand.

The shade cover provides some protection from harsh sun, wind and hail while letting enough light through for plant growth. Even more importantly, the cover provides an effective barrier against animal intruders, most notably possums. To some extent, insect pests such as aphids, thrips and cabbage white butterflies are excluded, as long as they are not introduced via seedlings planted into the Vegepod. By hanging a sticky trap from the top of the cover, we were able to monitor insect pest incursions, most of which were controlled by removing them by hand. We have also converted the system into

an effective plant-propagation unit by utilising a heavy-duty plastic cover that comes as an optional extra.

The same company has also released a 'budget' wicking option called the **Vegebag**, which has a collapsible design and handles that enable it to be moved easily. It holds 6 litres of water in the reservoir at the base of the bag, plus 80 litres of potting mix – enough to grow crops such as tomatoes. The optional professional-grade cover provides the same advantages as the Vegepod cover. Both of these systems are perfect for growing plants that sucker (such as mint), and they save up to 80 per cent on water use compared to growing in a conventional pot, while also ensuring that your plants never dry out.

Our trials with the WaterUps units gave us exceptional growth rates, while using only 20 per cent of the water needed for a conventional raised garden bed.

Creating an in-ground wicking bed

The innovative Australian company behind the WaterUps system (see pages 88–9) has created a new in-ground wicking bed called the Sub-Irrigation Channel (SIC). Each module is 1340 millimetres long x 470 millimetres wide x 160 millimetres deep, and it can be linked to as many other modules as desired to create a longer in-ground wicking-bed channel. WaterUps wicking tiles are then placed into the channel. When a number of modules are joined together using specially designed fittings, only one inlet pipe is required to fill the channel, regardless of the channel length.

The channel can be inserted into a trench, and then soil (or some other suitable growing medium, such as garden or potting mix, which can be bought in bulk from a landscape-supply business) is mounded on top of the channel. Alternatively, the channel can be placed on a flat surface, and soil can be mounded up over the top to create the growing bed. The great advantage of this in-ground system is that the bed can be made significantly wider than the 470-millimetre wide channel, because water will move laterally to the edges of the bed as well as vertically up through the soil.

For the trench system, follow these steps:

Step 1 Dig a trench that is 10 millimetres deeper than the SIC, ensuring that it is level or has the very slightest of falls for maximum storage in the below-ground reservoir.

Step 2 Lay a 10-millimetre layer of coarse gravel at the bottom of the trench, ensuring that it is level.

Step 3 Place WaterUps SIC wicking-bed modules into the prepared trench.

Step 4 Insert biochar into the wicking-bed modules.

Step 5 Make sure that the wicking legs are filled so the biochar is level with or slightly above the top of the legs. This ensures that the biochar will be in continuous contact with the geotextile fabric when it is installed in Step 7.

Step 6 Install a vertical inlet pipe to enable the SIC to be refilled with water.

Steps continued >

Step 1

Step 4

Step 2

Step 3

Step 5

Step 6

Step 7

Step 8

Step 10

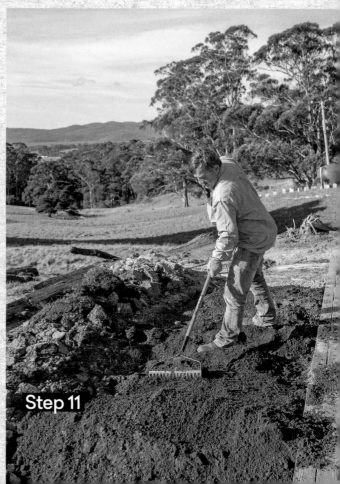

Step 11

Step 7 Cover the SIC with geotextile fabric to prevent silt from blocking the legs in the wicking-bed modules.

Step 8 Drill out the outlet hole in the SIC.

Step 9 Connect a length of garden hose to the overflow outlet.

Step 10 Backfill the SIC with a suitable soil mix.

Step 11 Level the soil mix prior to planting.

Step 12 The water inlet pipe is ready for a garden hose or similar to be inserted.

Step 13 The newly planted in-ground wicking bed is starting to thrive.

Step 9

Step 12

Step 13

Angus created a wicking bed on a Hobart rooftop using the WaterUps Sub-Irrigation Channel. To minimise its weight, a light material (perlite) was used in the wicking legs, while expanded clay was mixed with composted pine bark to create the growing medium.

4

FUTUREPROOF SOILS AND HOW TO CREATE THEM

Having access to irrigation water is, of course, vital to growing crops in areas with unreliable rainfall. We don't have a lot of control over rainfall; however, we do have a lot of control over the medium we use to grow our plants, whether that is soil, potting mix or something else. In this chapter, we will look at how to manage growing media to optimise water supply to the plants growing there. Let's start with soil, as this is by far the most common growing medium.

Soil texture is defined by the percentages of sand, silt and clay particles in your soil. It determines not only your soil's ability to hold moisture, but also how tightly the soil holds on to that water as well as the way water moves within wetted soil. Gardeners instinctively know that very sandy soils are not good at storing moisture and consequently have very good drainage, while very clayey soils are the opposite. These properties are modified by other factors, such as the soil's organic-matter content and the chemistry of the individual clay minerals that are present in any particular soil.

Clay gets a bad rap from many gardeners, but this poor reputation is not always deserved. It is quite a variable substance – there are about 30 separate clay minerals – and the type of clay minerals present determines whether you have a soil that is a dream or a nightmare for cultivating plants. Sand, on the other hand, is an inherently inert material with regard to soil chemistry, and its properties are much more predictable. The bottom line is that regardless of the mineral composition of your soil, there are various ways

that it can be improved in terms of storing and supplying moisture to plants. Let's explore how to work out your soil's texture and also how to improve it to suit the type of plants you are trying to grow or the growing system you are using.

DETERMINING SOIL TEXTURE

If you have never looked at your soil in detail, here is a simple and fun way to learn about one of the most important soil properties for delivering moisture to plant roots and therefore for creating a successful garden. It is the perfect way to get your kids away from the screens and into the outdoors as well.

Using a large glass jar, half fill it with a typical sample of your topsoil. Then fill the rest of the jar with water, and close the lid tightly. Shake the jar vigorously to completely separate all of the soil particles from one another. Then put the jar to one side, and allow the particles to settle. You will now see that the various soil particles have separated into layers according to their particle

---

The bottom line is that regardless of the mineral composition of your soil, there are various ways that it can be improved in terms of storing and supplying moisture to plants.

Selecting drought-tolerant Australian plants that suit your existing soil type is a smart way to design your garden.

SOIL TEXTURE JAR TEST

50–100% clay	
0–45% silt	
0–45% sand	

CLAYEY SOIL

10–30% clay
30–50% silt
25–50% sand

LOAMY SOIL

0–10% clay
0–10% silt
80–100% sand

SANDY SOIL

size. Sand, being the heaviest, settles to the bottom; silt, being the next biggest particle, forms the next layer. Clay is the lightest and sits above the silt, while on top you will find any organic matter that is present in the soil, as it is the lightest substance of all. By measuring the thickness of each layer, you can then accurately determine your soil's texture by working out the percentage by volume of each soil component.

Plants vary widely in their ability to grow in different soil textures, depending on how each species has evolved in its natural habitat. We are all familiar with plants that can grow in pure sand at the beach, such as spinifex grass and pigface (*Carpobrotus* species). At the other end of the spectrum are tough plants such as tea-trees (*Melaleuca* and *Leptospermum* species), which thrive in heavy soils that are rich in clay and hold lots of moisture. After working out our soil texture, we can choose species that are best adapted to grow in it. Alternatively, we can improve the soil if we want to grow species that are not well adapted to our current soil type.

Soil structure and its relationship to texture

One of the keys to optimising the supply of water to plant roots lies in soil structure – the way that the soil particles are arranged. When we have a structure with a wide variety of pore space sizes, from the smallest that retain water against the force of gravity, to the largest that are normally full of air, this means that the soil has good drainage. A soil that has a well-balanced structure can be easily cultivated to create a multitude of small soil crumbs that hold water within them and air between them. The small soil crumbs are known as **aggregates** or **peds**.

The key to creating the crumb structure lies in providing 'glue' that will stick the minute soil particles together to form aggregates that store water inside them and hold air between them. The 'glue' can be either mineral (via clay minerals in the soil) or organic in the form of humus, the ultimate breakdown product from composting. Sand and silt are chemically inert soil particles and by their very nature tend not

WORM POWER

One of our go-to strategies for soil improvement is to create earthworm populations in topsoil by adding worm castings (complete with egg capsules and living earthworms) to well-rotted manure (of any sort) and then spreading a 5–10-centimetre layer over the topsoil. We then place a 10-centimetre layer of woody mulch over the top to keep moisture levels even underneath, so the earthworms can work their magic. The worms feed on the manure and burrow down into the topsoil with it, enriching the soil's nutrient levels and cultivating the soil through their tunnelling activities, which in turn aids the soil's aeration and drainage. As they tunnel through the soil, the worms also deposit humus-rich manure (castings) that helps to enhance the formation of peds, thus improving soil structure.

to stick together, while clay is much more reactive chemically and can be amended with substances such as gypsum (calcium sulphate) that change the chemistry of the clay particles in a way that 'glues' them together to form peds. Consequently, humus is the best option for improving the water-holding capacity of a sandy or silty soil. For clayey soils, the subject is a bit more complicated, but it is fair to say that adding humus will also improve this soil structure.

When it comes to improving structure via substances such as gypsum, it is important to know that each of the dozens of different clay minerals behaves quite differently, so the effects of the addition of substances such as gypsum vary from soil to soil. Depending on the scale of the project, you may want to get your soil tested and seek expert advice from a soil specialist, who will come up with recommendations. For most gardeners, though, the annual addition of appropriate organic matter is not only the simplest way to build and maintain soil structure, but also a great way to fertilise plants with their nutrient requirements at the same time.

A spade is the ideal tool for cultivating soils if they have any degree of compaction.

IMPROVING WATER STORAGE AND DELIVERY TO PLANTS

One of the most important things you can do to futureproof your garden is to improve the ability of your soil (or other growing medium, such as potting mix) to store both water and nutrients. We mention nutrients as well as water here because this is the key to creating a healthy and thriving garden. Water is the means by which nutrients are transported from the soil and into the plant, so by ensuring an even and optimal water supply, we can create the best conditions for plant growth. Let's explore the various ways in which we can achieve our soil-improvement objectives.

Adding clay to sandy soils

Given that clay holds a lot of water and sand not so much, then the logical thing to do would be to add clay to a sandy soil. The theory is sound, but the devil lies in the detail: getting the very fine clay particles to mix evenly with sand can be a somewhat difficult exercise. However, it can be done if you choose the right type of clay mineral. The best options for this purpose are kaolinite and bentonite, as they are readily available and are effective at improving both moisture- and nutrient-holding capacity.

The clay particles can be worked through the soil easily if they are dry. Simply dig the clay through the soil with a garden fork, or – for a larger area – use a mechanical rotary hoe (they can be readily hired if you don't own one). If the clay is moist, it will be somewhat harder to get it into the sandy soil. In this case, put the clay into a bucket and half fill with water. Stir the water vigorously to get as much of the clay into suspension as possible, and then pour it evenly over the soil surface. This helps it to infiltrate and move down between the pore spaces in the sand.

Adding sand to clayey soils

Once again, the exercise of adding sand to clay is the difficult bit. The easiest and most effective option is to spread the sand over the topsoil in a layer about 5 centimetres deep, and then plough it in using a mechanical rotary hoe. It is particularly important to carry out the operation when the soil is moist but not wet. Dig a clod of soil and try to break it up with your fingers; if it crumbles, then it is the perfect time to cultivate. If it behaves like plasticine or is dry and brittle, then avoid cultivating it at all costs.

Far left: Dig a clay product such as kaolinite or bentonite through sandy soil with a garden fork to improve the soil's water-storage ability.

Left: If you can break up a clod of soil into crumbly pieces, then it is perfect for cultivation.

Adding organic matter to soils

When they see a black or very dark brown soil, most experienced gardeners proclaim that it is a rich, fertile soil. Why? Because they know that a high level of organic matter is perhaps the most important attribute of a soil in which plants grow well. Due to our very dry and sometimes hostile climate, Australian soils have some of the lowest levels of organic matter in the world, so any additions are almost always going to result in significant improvement.

There are three main reasons for using organic matter to amend your garden soil:

1   **To improve the structure of the soil** by creating a balance of different-sized pore spaces. The smaller pores hold water against the force of gravity and then act as a reservoir for plant growth; the larger pore spaces make soil more open and easier to cultivate, and improve its aeration and drainage. The organic materials used for this purpose are referred to as **soil conditioners**

and are most often made from low-nutrient organic matter, such as sawdust, pine bark and other woody materials. These materials need to be well composted before use as soil conditioners, otherwise they will draw nutrients out of the soil – leading to deficiencies in any plants growing in it. When properly composted, soil conditioners 'glue' soil particles together and also improve the water- and nutrient-holding ability of the soil.

2   **To slow down water loss** (and keep the soil temperature more even). Adding a layer of mulch accomplishes both tasks. Materials such as sawdust, pine bark and woodchips are most often used as mulches. They differ from soil conditioners in that they are generally made from woody materials that have not been composted, which means that they sit on the surface of the soil and remain intact for years. Lucerne hay and pea straw are much less woody than pine bark or woodchips, but they also function well

Above: Most plants – especially vegetables – grow best in a rich, fertile soil. If your soil lacks nutrients, you can improve it by incorporating organic matter.

as water-saving mulches; however, because they are much higher in nutrients, they tend to compost reasonably quickly (within months) in situ, enriching the soil with nutrients as well as humus to build good soil structure. These quick-composting mulches need to be replenished regularly.

3 **To fertilise the soil at the same time as improving its structure.**
For this we need organic materials such as animal manure, worm castings or high-quality composts that are made from raw ingredients with a high nutrient content.

We are constantly told in gardening books that the key to good soil management (as far as improving water retention goes) is to increase your soil's organic-matter content, and in broad terms this is very sound advice. However, the trick is to achieve this goal without creating any unwanted and unforeseen consequences. Depending on the source of your organic matter, you can create problems such as introducing weeds or robbing your soil of nutrients by using organic matter that is not fully broken down.

ORGANIC OPTIONS FOR MAXIMISING WATER EFFICIENCY

There is a multitude of organic materials that can be added to growing media to improve the infiltration and storage of water. Sometimes we are presented with a free locally sourced option, such as collecting manure from nearby farms, or we can make our own compost from household kitchen scraps. For large-scale garden projects, it may be more practical to buy ready-made organic soil amendments. Let's look at the most commonly available materials as well as their advantages and disadvantages.

Composts

Largely, it's the raw ingredients in compost that determine its value in enriching soil. As mentioned earlier, compost offers two major benefits when used as a soil improver: **soil conditioning** and sometimes (but not always) **fertilising**. Soil

Left: Composted pine bark is available in a range of particle sizes, ready to dig into a soil that needs improvement.

conditioning happens when the carbon in the various woody materials that go into a compost heap break down to produce an end product called humus; this is the stuff you really want in your soil, whatever its texture – sandy or clayey. Humus acts like glue, sticking together soil particles to create the crumb structure that in turn provides the desirable balance between air and water in the soil for plant growth. Humus also acts like a sponge, absorbing water and nutrients in the soil before releasing them back to the plant roots growing nearby.

Compost's fertilising ability depends on the nutrient content of the initial ingredients and also how the compost is made. Household compost will generally have a reasonable nutrient content if lots of moist kitchen scraps are added alongside lawn clippings and garden cuttings. However, if you mix in a couple of bags of a high-nutrient manure – such as that from chickens or ducks – this will absolutely ensure that your compost is nutrient-rich and ideal for digging into tired soils that need a lift. Commercial composts are made from many different ingredients and can vary widely in their nutrient content. Composts made from

lots of woody material supply few (if any) additional nutrients for plant growth and are best considered as soil conditioners (they will enhance water and nutrient storage, but should not be used as fertilisers). It is a good idea to read the label carefully when purchasing compost, as most manufacturers will give information about the nutritional value of their product.

While the advice to dig compost into your soil is almost universal in the gardening literature when talking about preparing soils, we don't often hear about the subject of **compost maturity**. Depending on the ingredients used to create your compost heap, they will take at least a couple of months to completely break down to a point where the compost offers the maximum benefit in improving your soil. The consequence of the compost not being fully broken down is that it will take away precious nutrients from nearby plant roots rather than add nutrients to the soil.

The best way to test whether your compost is indeed ready to use is to plant 20 or so fast-germinating seeds (such as radishes) in a compost-filled pot and see how many come up quickly. Look for high germination rates and healthy dark green seedlings; if neither of these

scenarios eventuate, you may need to add some extra nutrients to the compost so it reaches full maturity. Adding fresh or aged animal manure to the compost is one of the best and easiest methods to help your heap fully break down and provide maximum benefit in your soil.

The bottom line when it comes to adding compost to your soil is that you need to understand what it is you are trying to achieve so you choose the best compost for the job. If you want to boost your soil's water- and nutrient-holding capacity, then any mature compost will be useful. But if you wish to add nutrients as well, then you need to either purchase compost made from nutrient-rich materials or compost materials yourself in a way that preserves their nutrient value.

Coir (coconut) fibre

One of the great success stories of better sustainability in modern horticulture has been the widespread use of coir fibre derived from the processing of coconut husks when this crop is harvested in tropical areas of the world. It is now predominantly used as a major component of potting mixes and other growing media for plants. Prior to the adoption of coir fibre in the horticultural industry, peat moss was used as the 'sponge' that holds water and nutrients in soils and potting mixes. The problem with this is that peat moss is mined from peat bogs that take thousands of years to form (and therefore replenish), making the use of peat moss largely unsustainable in the long term.

Coir fibre has proven to be the perfect substitute for peat moss, as it can be milled to provide a range of particle sizes. It is important to ensure that coir fibre is not contaminated with salt (which sometimes blows onto stockpiles located in coastal areas where coconut palms are farmed). Selecting the appropriate particle size depends on your objective in using coir fibre: if it is mainly to build up a soil's water-holding capacity, then use the finer grades; if you want to improve drainage and aeration as well as water-holding capacity, then use chunkier particle sizes. Coir fibre often comes as compressed bricks, which need to be soaked in water to get the coir to expand to the point where it is ready to use.

Peat and sphagnum moss

These two materials have long been used to increase the water- and nutrient-holding capacity of soils and potting mixes; however, they have fallen out of favour recently because they are not a renewable resource (although they continue to be used in some horticultural circles). It is worth noting that the quality of these moss products is rather variable, depending on where they are mined, and this is another reason why their use is diminishing. They also have quite an acidic pH, and you will generally need to add a source of lime to counteract that acidity, especially in potting mixes.

Composted pine bark and sawdust

Plantation pines are one of our major sources of construction timber, but the bark is increasingly being valued in its own right as an ingredient in potting mixes. As it is high in carbon and very woody, pine bark must be well composted before it can be used successfully as an ingredient in potting mixes, otherwise it would strongly compete with plants for soil nutrients as the bark breaks down.

Composting the pine bark also allows us to mill it and separate it into a range of different particle sizes at the same time. By choosing the right particle size for our growing medium, we can create the optimal balance between air and

Opposite left: Feed your kitchen waste to the inhabitants of a worm farm, and you will soon have worm castings – a valuable soil improver.

Left: Sowing fast-germinating seeds (such as those of radish) is a great way to test whether your compost is ready to use. Here, the low-quality compost on the left shows poor germination compared to the good-quality potting mix used in the control on the right.

Far left: Eucalyptus sawdust or shavings need to be properly composted if they are to be used as a soil conditioner.

MUSHROOM COMPOST

water in the medium. The beauty of composted pine bark is that it is a renewable resource, as it comes from plantation timber. And there is absolutely no reason why we can't add it straight into the soil as well as using it in potting mix once it has been composted. Larger grades of chunky composted pine bark make an excellent long-term woody mulch on top of the soil.

Hardwood sawdust – a by-product from the milling of eucalyptus timber – is the most commonly composted sawdust available for horticulture in Australia. It is very high in carbon and low in nutrients, and therefore needs a lot of composting before it can be added to your soil. By adding what it lacks nutritionally during the composting process, we can turn the sawdust into relatively fine particles that will enhance the soil's water- and nutrient-holding capacity. In recent times, it has largely been replaced by coir fibre and composted pine bark; however, if you have a local source of hardwood sawdust, then it is worth your while to obtain some and compost it, as it can be a cost-effective option. Perform the seedling germination test mentioned on page 107 to ensure it is mature before use.

As the name suggests, this specialised type of compost is designed for commercial mushroom production. Once the rate of mushroom production starts to fall, the compost growing medium needs to be replaced if more mushrooms are to be grown, but the depleted compost still has excellent value as a soil amendment in many situations. It is usually high in lime and gypsum, and therefore can have a rather alkaline pH, making it particularly useful for neutralising acid soils. It also adds humus to improve a soil's water- and nutrient-holding capacity, and supplies some nutrients (those that are left over after the mushrooms have had their fill).

As it can sometimes have a high salinity level if there is a significant amount of fertiliser still present, it is best used as a one-off soil improver, particularly for clay soils – the relatively large calcium content in substances such as gypsum should help to break up soils with poor structure. Mushroom compost also contains relatively large quantities of organic matter and is a cost-effective way of conditioning your soil while also adding some nutrients, making it a good choice for intensive areas of the garden (such as the vegie patch).

Manures

Animal manures are excellent materials, as they usually add a lot of nutrients to the soil and help to improve soil structure. It is important to realise that there are major differences between various manures with regard to their balance of nutrients, as this depends on the diet and digestive system of the animal concerned. For instance, laying hens from commercial farms are often fed a diet high in grain and calcium to increase the strength of the eggshells, so their manure is often relatively high in calcium and therefore well suited to many intensive gardening situations (such as vegetable gardens and annual beds). On the other end of the scale, animals such as cows and sheep that feed on grass have manure with a nutrient content that is in the right proportions to maintain the needs of most plant species, so this manure can be used all over the garden.

Weed seeds can be a problem depending on what has been fed to the animal. Many types of manure are composted or processed now to ensure that no (or minimal) weed seeds are present. This ageing and/or composting process is also important in ensuring that the nutrient levels are not too high when the manure is applied to plants. Fresh manure can contain toxic levels of nutrient salts, so it is best to age or compost it for several weeks before using it in the garden.

WHY NOT TRY PERLITE?

A volcanic mineral rock, perlite is expanded by heating to create a lightweight material that is full of tiny pore spaces. This makes it quite good at storing water and also at wicking it upwards against the force of gravity. The rather coarse particle size of perlite also means that it allows plenty of aeration and drainage between the particles. It is a relatively inert substance that does not readily break down within the growing medium, so it is useful for situations where the growing medium does not get renewed very often, such as in a wicking bed or a roof garden. It comes in different grades depending on your purpose.

It is also important to note the health concerns around the use of manures. Cat and dog manure can harbour pathogens that are dangerous to humans and is best avoided when fertilising plants being grown for food.

Worm castings

Worm castings are the manure that comes from worms as they eat through their feedstock. Castings look and behave like topsoil, and are one of the best substances for increasing not only the water-holding capacity but also the fertility and nutrient-holding capacity of your soil. When used fresh, worm castings also introduce to the soil an array of beneficial microbes from their gut that also greatly improve soil biology.

Above left: Free-range chickens eat kitchen scraps and produce not only fresh eggs, but also a well-balanced fertiliser in the form of their manure.

Opposite: Composting the sawdust created during the milling of Tasmanian blue gum (*Eucalyptus globulus*) produces an excellent soil conditioner or potting mix ingredient.

Fresh worm castings are somewhat difficult to handle, as they are usually very fine in texture and full of moisture, and they tend to ooze rather than crumble.

We find that the best way to use them is to mix one part moist worm castings with nine parts water into a slurry that can be watered over the soil. This is a particularly effective way of improving the soil around existing trees and shrubs or for revitalising your indoor and outdoor potted plants. Drying out worm castings also works well, as they crumble readily when dry and can be easily dug into potting mix or soil.

Animal products

Blood and bone, hoof and horn, and fish meal are all manufactured from animal protein and bones. They are high in nitrogen, phosphorus and calcium but contain very little potassium. As they are expensive compared to other organic materials – and they contain relatively small amounts of humus when fully broken down – they are best considered as fertilisers rather than as soil conditioners, and should be used for intensive situations such as vegetable gardens. In summary, these products are a very expensive way to add organic matter to soils but an effective way to add particular nutrients that your soil lacks.

Biochar

We are all familiar with the red-hot coals of an open fire and how some of them remain as charred black lumps when the fire goes out, as opposed to the fine, grey, powdery ash that results if the fire is particularly intense. The 'black lumps' are a carbon-rich substance often known as biochar that results from the direct thermal decomposition of biomass (such as wood, leaves and bark) in an oxygen-depleted environment (which prevents combustion). The word 'biochar' is derived from the Greek *bios*, meaning 'life', and *char*, meaning the solid material left behind after the initial stage of combustion of carbonaceous material, such as wood. To make it at home, you can simply douse hot coals from an outdoor fire with water until they go out completely and then crush them up with a hammer. Commercially, special vessels are used to make biochar to ensure that it is produced as efficiently as possible.

Biochar is made up of a very stable chemical form of carbon that can remain in the soil for decades or even centuries. It is a porous material

Far left: Worms fed on kitchen scraps produce well-balanced and nutrient-rich castings that are a perfect soil improver.

Left: Sprinkling blood and bone over your soil is a great way to add nutrients, particularly phosphorus.

that acts like a sponge not only for water, but also for plant nutrients, and it provides a fertile site for the growth of plant roots and beneficial microbes as well. Another fantastic benefit is that the use of biochar helps to avoid the release of greenhouse gases, particularly carbon dioxide, which occurs when biomass is burned completely to ash. It is a win-win situation for our environment: biochar helps to limit the production of greenhouse gases, and at the same time it also makes your trees and shrubs grow faster so they absorb more carbon dioxide from the atmosphere.

When using biochar, it is important to activate it with nutrients to get the full benefit. Indeed, if we add raw biochar to the soil, it will absorb nutrients initially – and thus biochar may compete with your plants for nutrients. To avoid this, simply activate the biochar with a suitably nutrient-rich organic fertiliser, such as a slurry of worm castings or some homemade compost with plenty of decomposed kitchen scraps (this will also introduce lots of beneficial microbes that will thrive in the environment around the biochar in the soil). The beauty of this approach is that as well as supplying nutrients, the biochar also stores a lot more water in the soil to supply the plants' growing needs.

The use of biochar as a soil improver dates back to prehistoric farming practices that were carried out in the Amazon River basin. The first peoples of the Amazon River basin apparently produced biochar by setting fire to agricultural waste in either pits or trenches and then quickly covering it with soil so it smouldered. The legacy of these unique farming practices has lived on through the creation of a very interesting soil type called *terra preta*, which is predominantly formed by human intervention (a soil type referred to by soil scientists as an **anthroposol**) through the incorporation of large quantities of plant charcoal (biochar) into agricultural soil. Studies of these soils have demonstrated that the biochar carbon has remained stable for hundreds of years, and a high level of soil fertility has been maintained. Talk about futureproofing your soil!

Above left: Mixing biochar with worm castings creates a slow-release nutrient source for your soil that will also build up its water-holding capacity.

Above right: You can reduce the bushfire-fuel load around your property by turning dead branches, twigs and leaves into homemade biochar.

Making biochar

There are many different ways to make biochar, from simply digging a pit and creating the biochar in the soil, to the more complex processes of industrial-scale systems. Here we are utilising a stainless-steel biochar 'cone' that is portable and very easy to use.

Step 1 Carbon-rich material is the perfect raw ingredient for making biochar. Here, Angus has collected dry bark, dead twigs and branches as well as leaf litter from the eucalypt forest on his farm.

Step 2 Start a fire in the base of the cone, then add the carbon-rich material in a number of layers.

Step 3 Allow each layer to catch on fire and flame up before covering it with the next layer.

Step 4 Rake the burning material every so often to ensure that there is even combustion within the cone.

Step 5 Allow the fire to burn until the material turns black. It is critically important that the fire does not burn so long that the material turns into powdery grey ash.

Step 6 Use copious amounts of water to douse the cone once the majority of material has blackened and become biochar. Rake over the embers a few times while hosing them down to ensure that they have stopped smouldering completely.

Steps continued >

Step 1

Step 4

Step 2

Step 3

Step 5

Step 6

Step 7 Spread the biochar out on tarps to dry.
If you live on acreage, making your own biochar is
feasible and helps to reduce bushfire-fuel loads.
However, if you do not have the space to produce
your own biochar, it is also available to buy from
garden centres, nurseries and hardware stores.

MULCHES

The role of mulches in reducing water loss from soils is very well documented, so mulch should be a major part of your strategy for creating a water-smart soil. A wide range of organic and inorganic materials can be used as mulch, including:

* hay/straw
* coir (coconut fibre)
* woodchips
* pine bark
* shredded sugarcane
* homemade compost
* newspaper and/or cardboard (preferably with a woody mulch on top)
* sawdust
* oyster shells
* washed seaweed and seagrass
* gravel/pebbles
* synthetic weed mats.

Regardless of the material you choose, remember that the larger the particle size the better: the mulch will be able to trap pockets of air to create an insulating layer on top of the soil. This not only conserves moisture in the soil by decreasing evaporation, but also suppresses weed growth and keeps the soil temperature more even, preventing extremes that may be harmful to plant growth.

Organic or inorganic?

Depending on the material you are using for your mulch, it can also potentially play a role in building up your soil's organic-matter content, which in turn will increase its water-holding capacity. Lucerne hay and pea straw are both relatively nutrient-rich mulch materials that will break down fairly quickly at the interface between the soil and mulch, adding vital humus to the layer where plant roots are most active. You will also generally observe a significant increase in earthworm activity under these mulches, which further enhances their beneficial effects. We refer to these types of mulches as 'feeder' mulches because they break down readily and literally 'feed' the soil with humus and nutrients.

TRAPS WITH ORGANIC MATERIALS

Not all organic materials are equal when it comes to soil amendments. Some materials contain weed seeds, some are too acidic or alkaline, and some repel water and are hard to wet when they dry right out. Most of these things are impossible to judge by looking at the material with the naked eye. If you want to be safe, look for the Australian Standards logo on products you purchase (or ask for certification if buying in bulk from a landscape yard), as the standards specify quality parameters that ensure these materials should be free of any major problems. To learn more, search for AS 4454-2012 Composts, Soil Conditioners and Mulches on the Australian Standards website.

Woodchips

Pine bark

Sugarcane mulch

Homemade compost

Newspaper/cardboard

Oyster shells

Washed seaweed/seagrass

Gravel/pebbles

Synthetic weed mats

Shredded garden clippings produced during pruning and allowed to dry out make a good-quality weed-free mulch.

Organic materials that are not composted – such as woodchips, pine bark and sawdust – are particularly suitable as mulch around permanent plantings such as shrubberies, because they last a lot longer on the soil surface than other organic mulches. For these woody mulches, you need to be careful not to mix the mulch into the soil, as it will rob the soil of nutrients as it tries to break down. The great advantage of these materials is that they will take a long time to break down and therefore do not need to be replaced often. They are also excellent at suppressing weeds.

It is also feasible to use composted materials as mulch, but these will need to be topped up regularly. They will probably need to be weeded as well, because weed seeds are likely to blow in from the surrounding environment, germinate in the mulch and grow quite readily.

Inorganic mulches such as coarse gravel are a particularly useful option in fire-prone areas because they are not flammable. They also offer a permanent option that will last indefinitely. Be careful not to allow soil or compost to contaminate the inorganic mulch, as this will encourage weed growth.

The colour of your mulch is also an important choice, as light-coloured materials reflect the sun's rays better than darker materials and will be more effective at preserving moisture in the soil. Ultimately, your choice of mulch material will come down to cost and local availability, so keep an open mind about repurposing and recycling materials that could be effective as mulch.

Left: Pebbles come in different size grades and colours, but they are all suitable for use as mulch.

Inorganic mulches such as coarse gravel are a particularly useful option in fire-prone areas as they are not flammable.

ARE HYDROGELS THE ANSWER?

A modern option for increasing water-holding capacity in soil is the addition of hydrogels (water-storing crystals), which swell to many times their original size when water is added; they then slowly release the water as the soil dries out. These substances are also used in other contexts, such as in disposable nappies where they absorb urine and keep the baby dry over an extended time.

There is no question that these substances are good at absorbing water, but we have had trouble finding data on how effective these substances are in supplying the water back to plants. Another issue is that water-storing crystals are made from various artificial chemicals, often polyacrylamides. We are not in favour of their use on a variety of health and environmental grounds – we do not think it is worth taking the risk of introducing artificial chemicals into our growing environments when there are so many natural and organic alternatives that can be sourced, often for free. While it appears that there are no acute problems caused by these chemicals, it is difficult to be certain that they do not cause any long-term problems through unintended consequences. There are so many natural substances that we can add to our growing media to improve water efficiency, so why use materials that may end up being damaging either to you or to the environment?

5

DESIGNING A FUTUREPROOF LANDSCAPE

In Chapter 2, we looked at how to harvest rainwater for bulk storage in tanks, ponds and dams – the reverse of 'saving for a rainy day'. These water-storage solutions, along with pipes and pumps to deliver the water to your plants, are very important to have if you live in a climate where the capacity to irrigate is necessary for some or all of the year – usually in summer in Australia.

This is particularly important if you want to grow your own food, as most edible plants will suffer badly if they run out of water at any stage of the crop cycle. We can greatly lessen the need for irrigation if we take advantage of rainfall to capture most of that natural precipitation in our soil profile.

We learned in Chapter 4 how to improve our soil from a water-storage point of view, so our challenge in this chapter is to create a landscape that will funnel as much water as possible into our improved soil. We do this by redirecting surface and subsurface water, as well as slowing it down, so that more of the rainwater has a chance to infiltrate and be stored in soil rather than running off and away from our garden.

It is rather crazy to think that stormwater has traditionally been viewed as a problem to be funnelled away as quickly and efficiently as possible to our various waterways, such as creeks, rivers and oceans. Unfortunately, rather than solving a problem, channelling stormwater away actually creates greater problems – as it makes its way towards our waterways, it picks up the various pollutants (such as plastics and chemicals) that are prevalent in human-dominated environments. Even dog manure that is deposited as you take the family pet for a walk can create toxic algal blooms if it is left to wash away in the next storm.

Wouldn't it be so much better for our environment and us if we regarded stormwater as a valuable resource to be harvested on-site? Then it could be used to irrigate edible and ornamental gardens, to fight bushfires or to create ponds and dams that are both water features and habitats for wildlife. There are a number of ways that we can improve the capture of stormwater in our gardens, with varying levels of sophistication and expense.

It is critical to note that rain and stormwater **must** be retained on-site in a way that does not allow water to accumulate in the soil within a metre of any buildings, particularly your house. Most of us have heard of 'rising damp', where subsurface moisture in the soil banks up against the foundations and walls of a building or flows under a building and cannot get away, resulting in that water often moving into the building's structure – which in turn can cause extremely serious damage that is very expensive to remediate. With its tendency to retain more water, clayey soil is particularly problematic in this regard.

We redirect surface and subsurface water so that more of the rainwater can be stored in soil rather than running off and away from our garden.

Stormwater and subsurface water can be redirected to other parts of your garden via flexible agricultural pipe.

The issue of rising damp is readily addressed by the installation of a suitable subsurface drainage system. Depending on your situation, it may be a very wise investment to seek expert advice from a suitably qualified civil engineer to make sure there is no conflict between the garden and the long-term structural integrity of your buildings (particularly if you have a sloping site with a clayey soil, or reside on one of the much smaller blocks of land that now proliferate in many cities and towns). We will cover the basic principles of subsurface drainage later in this chapter, but it is worth emphasising that diverting rainwater into tanks for irrigation will help to alleviate drainage problems, particularly during major rainfall events.

SWALES AND MOUNDS

Depending on the existing topography of your land, it may be possible to create a series of raised mounds and shallow swales (ditches) that will stop most – if not all – of the stormwater from leaving your property. This will give the stormwater time to soak into your soil, where it can then be stored for use by your plants while waiting for the next lot of rainfall.

The easiest way to increase your ability to harvest water in a flat area of the garden is to dig out the topsoil and pile it up so you create a series of undulating mounds and swales. These will not only catch and store water, but also offer interesting planting opportunities. The stormwater collects in the swales, creating moist zones at the base of the mounds that suit moisture-loving species, while the tops of the mounds are perfect for plants that need well-drained soil. Once again, let us emphasise that retaining stormwater on-site must be done in a way that does not result in subsurface moisture accumulating in the soil near your building foundations.

Creating highs and lows

If you are not already familiar with your soil profile, then dig a hole and observe the different horizons

Above left: With the right design, an artificial mound can be a stunning and self-watering landscape feature.

Above right: A swale has been used to create a pond. The bed of sunflowers next to the pond soaks up the water via capillary action.

(layers). Generally, you will find a reasonably well-drained layer of topsoil over a heavier clay subsoil. If this is the case, then you can simply dig out the topsoil and mound it up, leaving behind a shallow swale that will collect water during rainfall; the water will pool in the swale and gradually soak into the soil below and beside it. Another option for creating mounds is to bring in a suitable imported soil rather than digging out your existing topsoil.

If you have a perfectly flat site, then the mounds and swales can be positioned in whatever way takes your fancy. On the other hand, if you are on a sloping site, then the mounds should follow the contours of your property so the stormwater will collect behind them. Depending on the topography and size of your property, it may be more feasible to construct a series of overlapping mounds and swales down the slope. This will slow down the flow of the water and eventually stop it leaving your property before it creates pollution problems down the line. And, of course,

by creating reservoirs of moisture in your soil, you will be encouraging your trees and shrubs to send their roots much deeper, which will greatly assist them during dry spells.

Mounds and swales also offer opportunities for planting diversity in your garden, as the altered landscape generates a series of micro-environments. The tops of the mounds are ideal for plant species that need very good drainage, while the base of the mounds will obviously be moister, especially after rainfall, so would be suitable for plants that don't mind wet feet. Depending on the topography of your garden, you may also choose to create mini watercourses through the swales as a way of slowing water flow even further in torrential downpours. Filling the swales with attractive rocks will prevent erosion in extreme weather events.

OTHER STORMWATER-RETENTION IDEAS

Apart from the obvious idea of collecting rainwater by reshaping the surface of your landscape, there are other less visible things you can do to increase the amount of water that penetrates and is then stored in your soil. In Angus's experience, one of the most overlooked factors is encouraging more water to infiltrate your soil, so let's start there.

Improving water infiltration

Surface run-off increases significantly if rainwater has trouble infiltrating the soil surface. In extreme cases, soils become hydrophobic and actually repel water, with little hope of the precious moisture reaching your plant roots. To establish whether you have a hydrophobic soil, simply pour a glass of water onto your soil. If it forms spherical droplets that sit stubbornly on the soil surface, then you have a hydrophobic soil.

There is a host of soil-wetting agents available for an instant fix (see page 62), or you could cultivate your soil and incorporate a moisture-absorbing material (such as coir fibre) into the very top layer. If you then place a layer of mulch over your soil, it will help to slow the movement of water across the soil and give the water a greater chance to soak in – even the worst hydrophobic soils will eventually absorb moisture given enough time. Mulching is also a very important method for minimising evaporation from the soil surface (see Chapter 4).

If you have a sloping site, create a little moat above and adjacent to long-lived perennials, trees and shrubs. Fill up the moat when watering, and the water will gradually overcome the slow infiltration rate. Similarly, when it rains, the moat will fill up and the water will eventually soak in where it is needed most.

Soil compaction can also stop water from entering the soil. This problem is especially prevalent around newly constructed homes, where the movement of heavy machinery has compacted the soil around the building, and is compounded if the soil is clay-based. Cultivating the soil well, adding appropriate ameliorants (such as mature compost and/or gypsum) and mulching to a depth of 10 centimetres will generally alleviate this issue. A good way to test if your soil is suffering from over-compaction is to try to poke a screwdriver into the surface. If you

Left: Granules of a soil-wetting agent are sprinkled onto a hydrophobic soil to improve water infiltration.

need to use a lot of force to push the screwdriver into the soil, then it is time to cultivate. There are even special tools used in turf maintenance that will remove tiny soil cores to relieve compaction in lawns.

Creating French drains and storage wells

Another option for retaining stormwater is to create French drains or storage wells (sumps) in your soil that can store the water below ground level and allow it to gradually soak into your subsoil. It is then available for plant growth or to simply recharge the supply of water stored in your subsoil. Remember, though, that you must not allow water to accumulate around the walls and foundations of buildings.

The French drain is a very simple concept that has been used for hundreds of years to distribute stormwater or greywater from septic tank overflows into the subsoil. Perforated pipes or other structures are placed in ditches and surrounded by gravel to allow water to drain easily. The pipes are encased in a geotextile fabric 'sock' that helps to prevent fine particles from getting in and clogging the system.

Products such as soakwells can be used in a similar way to a French drain, particularly in gardens with sandy soils. A soakwell is a simple plastic container that is connected to a downpipe and buried in the soil. Stormwater flows down the pipe and accumulates in the soakwell, then gradually seeps out from slots in the sides of the container and into the surrounding subsoil. The soakwell can be positioned so that it provides irrigation water to nearby trees and shrubs. An overflow can be installed to ensure that if the soakwell fills completely during a very large storm event, then the excess water can drain away where it won't cause any damage. This is particularly important if your garden has heavier soils.

When siting French drains and storage wells, keep them downslope from buildings that might be affected badly by rising damp caused by subsurface moisture. It is also important to locate soakwells at least a metre from the house, especially if there is any appreciable amount of clay in the soil profile.

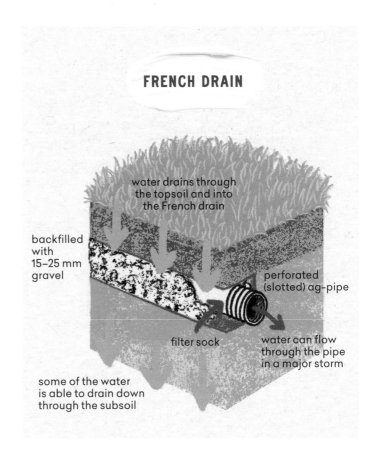

FRENCH DRAIN

water drains through the topsoil and into the French drain

backfilled with 15–25 mm gravel

perforated (slotted) ag-pipe

filter sock

water can flow through the pipe in a major storm

some of the water is able to drain down through the subsoil

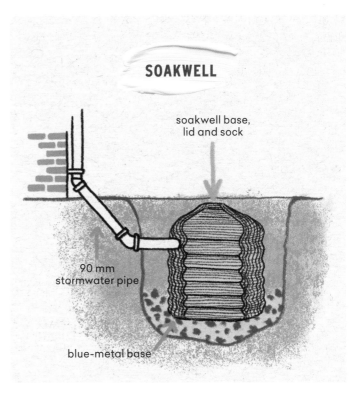

SOAKWELL

soakwell base, lid and sock

90 mm stormwater pipe

blue-metal base

PREMAYDENA COMMUNITY GARDEN

Angus has been heavily involved in this southern Tasmanian project for several years. On a sloping site, a series of surface and subsurface drains has been created to channel stormwater into a large dam at the base of the main slope as well as to facilitate water soaking into the soil as it makes its way down the slope. Rocks have been used to create dry creek beds that can channel water while minimising erosion during heavy downpours; the native succulent pigface (*Carpobrotus rossii*) has been planted to stabilise the terraced banks that follow the contours running across the slope.

A solar-powered pump moves water back up the slope when the sun is shining. This water is stored in large tanks at the top of the slope and gravity-fed back down the hill to irrigate the various gardens, including an edible garden full of water-efficient wicking beds. By assessing the site when planning infrastructure for water collection, storage and distribution, Angus and the other gardeners were able to create a system that is as sustainable as possible.

Depending on your situation, obtaining knowledgeable advice from a water specialist (such as an irrigation or water-pump expert) is a great way to ensure that you create a system with the water pressure you need to service your landscape efficiently. They can help to design a system that will meet your individual requirements.

Growing rain gardens

A rain garden is one that uses plants and soil media (either natural or artificial) as a biofiltration system to retain stormwater on-site. This reduces flow rates and therefore potential erosion, as well as remediating contaminants that may have been picked up by the stormwater. Any water that exits the rain garden can be a valuable resource for various purposes but is particularly well suited as backup irrigation water for the rest of the garden.

Rain gardens are excellent for sites that have significant catchment areas – particularly hard surfaces such as roads, roofs and paving – and hence generate sizeable volumes of stormwater, which is often contaminated with things such as hydrocarbons. They help to reduce the amount of pollutants entering public waterways, particularly in heavily populated urban areas.

When tough wetland-edge plants such as rushes and sedges, as well as water-loving shrubs such as bottlebrushes (*Callistemon* species) and honey myrtles (*Melaleuca* species), are planted in a specially constructed garden, they act as excellent biofilters to prevent fuel spillages, oil drips, particulate matter from vehicle tyres and other sorts of contaminants from moving into the wider environment.

Bottlebrushes (*Callistemon* species) are often found in habitats that are periodically waterlogged.

Rain gardens are an effective way of turning the problem of excess stormwater into a beautiful landscape feature.

RESIDENTIAL RAIN GARDEN

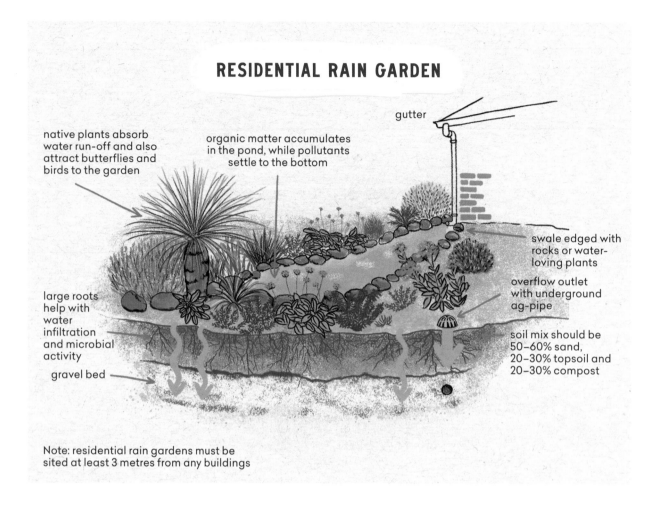

gutter

native plants absorb water run-off and also attract butterflies and birds to the garden

organic matter accumulates in the pond, while pollutants settle to the bottom

swale edged with rocks or water-loving plants

overflow outlet with underground ag-pipe

large roots help with water infiltration and microbial activity

gravel bed

soil mix should be 50–60% sand, 20–30% topsoil and 20–30% compost

Note: residential rain gardens must be sited at least 3 metres from any buildings

Constructing a rain garden can be broken down into five simple steps:

1   **Choose a low-lying spot** in the landscape into which significant amounts of stormwater can drain. Ensure that the site is several metres away from any buildings.

2   **If you have a clayey soil,** then you do not need to amend it (clay holds stormwater in the biofiltration system and aids in its purification). If you have a sandy or loamy soil, add plenty of well-rotted compost or manure to build up the soil's water-holding capacity.

3   **Channel stormwater** to the rain-garden area through either surface or subsurface drains.

4   **Select plants that thrive** with periodic stormwater inundation. There are a host of Australian plants that grow naturally alongside rivers and creeks, such as mat rushes (*Lomandra* species), flax lilies (*Dianella* species), honey myrtles (*Melaleuca* species) and tea-trees (*Leptospermum* species). Choose compact forms that are not going to produce invasive root systems, such as thyme-leaf honey myrtle (*Melaleuca thymifolia*) and *Leptospermum rotundifolium* 'Julie Ann'.

5   **Use stonework** to create an aesthetic and also to help prevent erosion during a really big storm.

KEYLINE FARMING AND PERMACULTURE

These are two fascinating examples of land-management systems that have been developed in Australia and incorporate the sort of sustainability and futureproofing principles and practices we are focusing on in this book. The difference with these two philosophies is that they are generally (but not exclusively) practised on a large landscape scale (rather than in small suburban gardens). An Australian farmer and engineer, the late P.A. Yeomans, developed the concept of keyline farming, and he released his first book (*The Keyline Plan*) on the subject in 1954. Many of Yeomans' principles were adopted by David Holmgren, one of the founders of the more recent land-management system known as **permaculture**.

At the heart of both systems is a holistic way of looking at a landscape and particularly its water (and other natural resources). Like the mound and swale system outlined earlier in this chapter, keyline farming and permaculture work on the principle of trying to harvest as much rain and stormwater as possible within the landscape. That water resource is then stored either in dams or directly in the soil by creating an environment where most of the stormwater has a chance to soak into the soil rather than running off into waterways.

Usually, for both keyline farming and permaculture, an overall property plan is created to optimise water resources. An ingenious idea from keyline farming is to build one or more dams at the highest topographical elevation, so that water can be gravity-fed to lower dams or areas of the farm for irrigation during dry spells.

A word of caution when designing holistic landscape systems: you are likely to need permission from government bodies such as your local council before constructing dams. You also need to ensure that it is legal to divert water flows so they stay on your property rather than reaching your neighbours' properties downstream.

P.A. Yeomans and his family, as well as the many current practitioners of permaculture, have made available online a great wealth of information on their systems. The concepts

At the heart of both systems is a holistic way of looking at a landscape and particularly its water.

are very detailed, and it is beyond the scope of this book to explain the ideas in depth. However, Angus would encourage you to research both systems for tips and approaches that you can adapt to your own garden and its design. Two excellent places to start are the book entitled *Water for Every Farm: Yeomans Keyline Plan* and the Permaculture Australia website (https://permacultureaustralia.org.au).

Above: The keyline farming system revolves around capturing and storing water at strategic points in the landscape that enable water-efficient gravity-fed irrigation.

A spring-fed dam on Angus's property provides a permanent water source that can be pumped to higher points on the farm. This allows for gravity-fed irrigation and liquid feeding of tree and shrub plantings at strategic times of the year.

A very important idea – especially in hot and dry climates – is to plant windbreaks that will slow down air movement over your garden. Some air movement is good to keep fungal leaf diseases from running rampant; however, strong winds greatly increase evapotranspiration rates and lead to demand for much more water if plants are to maintain growth or, indeed, survive in drought conditions. Ideally, if your property is large enough, plant a line of shrubs beside a line of trees to funnel wind over your garden rather than through it. Choose tough species that are adaptable to your local environment. Your local nursery or garden club will often have a wealth of experience and advice on this subject.

CREATING SHADE

It may sound obvious, but creating shade is a great way to lessen water loss through evaporation (and transpiration where plants are involved). A shadehouse is a simple and cost-effective way to create a semi-protected environment that will significantly reduce water loss from whatever is inside it. There are many plant species that thrive in shady conditions, such as ferns and bromeliads. However, a shadehouse can also be a temporary solution for protecting flowering plants that are in danger of being badly damaged by extreme weather conditions such as heatwaves and strong winds.

Shadecloth is available in various grades that provide different shade levels, and your choice will depend on what you will be growing under it. Retractable screens that can be operated either electronically or by hand can be used to create protected environments for plants on decks and courtyards during extreme weather conditions.

Sunburn of flowers, fruits, leaves and stems can seriously affect plants, especially if the hot sun appears suddenly after a period of relatively mild weather. Umbrellas, temporary shadecloth screens or even leafy branches of plants that have been pruned recently can all be used to quickly protect sensitive plants from unforeseen extreme conditions.

TOO MUCH WATER

We spend a lot of time and money on drought-proofing our gardens with rainwater tanks and irrigation systems, but what about the opposite situation – when it just won't stop raining? Or when subsurface water from springs or neighbouring properties flows through your land? The long-term consequences of water banking up against buildings can lead to very expensive remediation works. In the worst-case scenario, stormwater cannot drain away fast enough; the soil becomes totally saturated and may even go under water entirely, in which case we have a **flood**.

Above left: If you don't have the space or budget for a shadehouse, then try one of the versatile shading solutions for small spaces. This one from Australian company Flexi Garden Frames can be adapted to various sizes and spaces, such as this wicking bed.

Far left: Low-lying areas can easily become boggy for long periods. Many plant species find it difficult to grow in this wet soil environment.

Left: The sudden death of plants – often due to root rot – is a frequent consequence of extended soil waterlogging.

Flooding can, of course, cause catastrophic damage to a property, particularly if buildings become inundated. The consequences in the garden can also be disastrous, with destruction of hard landscaping such as sheds, garden beds and pathways. The impact on plants can be equally devastating, and it may go on for weeks after a flooding event or long periods of wet weather. Prolonged waterlogging often leads to conditions that favour the development of root-rotting fungi, and it is not uncommon to see plants die suddenly in the days, weeks and months after a flood.

The most obvious thing in a flood is the stormwater above ground. Ensuring that your gutters and surface drains have the capacity to cope with the peak surge of stormwater during heavy downpours is critical, whether you are building a new property or retrofitting an old one. To calculate how much water will be shed by a hard surface during a storm (and will need to be carried away by gutters or drains), multiply the surface area in square metres by the amount of storm rainfall in metres. This gives the amount of water being shed by the surface in cubic metres. Convert that to litres by multiplying the number of cubic metres by 1000.

For instance, a typical suburban block of land may have a surface area of 150 square metres (excluding the buildings). If a heavy storm usually dumps 50 millimetres (0.05 metres) of rain, then the average run-off per storm will be 150 x 0.05 = 7.5 cubic metres of water = 7.5 x 1000 = 7500 litres of water. The Bureau of Meteorology publishes information online about rainfall events (such as storms), so it is a good starting point for your research.

Once the pore spaces in the soil are full (in other words, the soil is saturated), the soil will start to shed water along the surface (or it will pond on a flat surface). In addition, it will also start to shed water below the soil surface, through the soil profile. This is subsurface drainage, and it is important to know where this subsurface drainage ends up, as this can help us to work out how to channel excess water, hopefully to somewhere useful.

Water draining through the soil profile will either be retained by the soil or reach and become part of the water table (constantly water-saturated ground). A heavy rainfall event will usually cause the water table to rise, and eventually – if enough water is added to the soil – the water table may reach the surface

and create a body of free water above the soil. When this happens, the soil remains totally saturated for as long as it takes for the water table to recede after the rainfall event ceases.

The good news is that a basic understanding of the excess-water issue can inform your decisions about what you might attempt at a do-it-yourself level, and when you might need an expert (such as a structural engineer) to design a drainage system that will alleviate the problem.

How to fix waterlogging

If you often have complete flooding or temporary waterlogging of your garden after a storm, then the best solution is to install a drainage system that not only stops the problem, but also takes that stormwater to where it can be beneficial. This drainage system should be designed to cope with the maximum downpour that you are likely to experience (using the information and formula on page 137). There are two ways

Far left: Bare soil areas are prone to erosion during heavy rain events. Installing a range of efficient surface and subsurface drainage systems – coupled with the establishment of vegetation – is a cost-effective way to mitigate any damage.

SELECT WATER-LOVING PLANTS

As well as taking water away from one area and directing it to where it is not going to cause problems, we can also ensure that our plant choices suit the micro-environments that we find in our garden. Earlier in this chapter we talked about rain (biofiltration) gardens that can be installed in low-lying areas to absorb and purify stormwater. Designers of rain gardens usually choose plant species that have evolved to tolerate occasional wet feet. Australian plants such as bottlebrushes (*Callistemon* species), honey myrtles (*Melaleuca* species) and tea-trees (*Leptospermum* species) typically grow alongside creeks and rivers, and they are perfect for areas that are likely to experience periodic waterlogging.

Tea-tree (*Leptospermum* species)

to improve your garden's drainage, so let's look at both of them.

As the name suggests, **surface drainage** diverts water that flows over the soil surface without soaking in. Surface drainage can be as simple as using various types of ploughs to create furrows along a contour line. These furrows intercept stormwater as it flows down a slope and provide more opportunity and surface area for the water to soak in. Permanent surface drainage can be created using various types of drains, from concrete spillways to gutter-type drains that can be embedded in driveways and paths to intercept stormwater. Once again, we emphasise that this must be designed so any water kept on-site does not impinge on building foundations.

Earlier in this chapter we covered some of the best options for **subsurface drainage**: French drains and soakwells (which act as sumps in the soil). Both options can be engineered to keep the stormwater on-site and allow it to soak into your soil (hopefully your garden design allows this water to be utilised well). If we have excessive amounts of water in the subsoil, or if it is flowing underground and potentially damaging buildings, then we need to divert the underground flow of water by linking subsurface drains to a municipal stormwater system that will safely guide the water away from where it may do harm. There are legal issues around diverting stormwater onto surrounding properties, so working with a licensed plumber or civil engineer will ensure that you do not cause any unforeseen problems for yourself or your neighbours.

Note that it is much easier to create a drainage system before your garden is planted than to try to retrofit it. A careful site assessment of topography, climatic data (such as rainfall amount and intensity) and soil type – and how these factors interact with the hard and soft landscapes – will inform your decisions on the design of the drainage system.

AG-PIPES TO THE RESCUE

The same slotted PVC pipe that is often used to create French drains can also be used to move water off-site. The purpose of agricultural drainage pipes ('ag-pipes') is to drain away any water that is in the ground. We have been using an innovative Australian product called Stretch Ag-Pipe that comes as a compressed tube. It is pulled out and extended, and it can bend around corners and hold that shape, making installation easy and flexible.

The Stretch Ag-Pipe (or a similar product) is placed into a trench that has a thin layer of 10–20-millimetre gravel on the bottom, and then the trench is backfilled with the same type of gravel so any water moving underground through the soil will be intercepted. Water seeps into the trench and through the gravel; it enters the ag-pipe through slots and is carried away. The pipe has a stocking-like geotextile fabric filter around it to prevent it from being clogged with any soil particles that are washed down through the gravel.

When installing ag-pipes to remove excess groundwater, it is vitally important to ensure that there is a fall of at least one in a hundred – preferably one in fifty – that is consistent along the entire trench in the direction of water flow. If there are any spots where the fall is not consistent, water can move out of the ag-pipe as well as into it, defeating the purpose of installing the ag-pipe. Water in and around the pipe should always be able to drain by gravity along the trench.

Position agricultural drains no closer than 1 metre from your house footings. Use solid pathways or grade the ground away from your house for the first metre. Never run slotted ag-pipe drains **under** your house, as any water flowing back out of the ag-pipe and into the soil can disturb the foundations. The other obvious point is that the low end of the pipe should discharge away from any buildings into either a garden area or a legal discharge point from your property.

A careful site assessment of topography, climatic data and soil type will inform your decisions on the design of the drainage system.

Installing an ag-pipe subsurface drain

Regardless of their size, subsurface drains are best installed during the construction phase of landscape establishment. It is worth consulting a plumber or a landscape contractor to ensure that the design of your drainage system not only is effective, but also complies with any legislative requirements, because changing the movement of water between adjoining properties can be fraught with problems. Once you have the design right, much of the project can be 'do it yourself'.

Step 1 Dig a trench that allows a suitable fall for water to move from the top of the subsurface drain to the lowest point.

Step 2 We used stretch ag-pipe, a highly versatile product that is – unlike traditional ag-pipe – completely flexible. It can bend around any obstacle, making installation quick and easy.

Step 3 Expand the ag-pipe to the required length. It will retain its shape during installation.

Step 4 Cover the ag-pipe with a filter sock, as this helps to stop sediment from blocking the pipe.

Step 5 Use joiners to create extended ag-pipe runs.

Step 6 Overlap the filter socks from each length to completely enclose joined ag-pipes.

Steps continued >

Step 1

Step 4

Step 2

Step 3

Step 5

Step 6

Step 7 Carefully lay the joined ag-pipes in the pre-prepared trench.

Step 8 Stormwater from a small shed is being diverted into the subsurface drain, along with stormwater that is moving underneath the soil surface from upslope.

Step 9 Backfill the drain with coarse gravel to facilitate the flow of water into the ag-pipe.

Step 10 A gardener's work is never done.

Step 7

Step 8

Step 9

Step 10

6

PLANTING TECHNIQUES

Plants are remarkably adaptable organisms, and we can use this to our advantage when creating our futureproof garden. How we acclimatise our plants even before they go in the ground – and the way we plant them – can affect their establishment and subsequent survival.

We can train our plants not only to seek out the water that is often available deeper in the soil profile, but also to need less water from artificial irrigation, simply by encouraging and enhancing their natural growth patterns.

ACCLIMATISING PLANTS TO LESS WATER

This applies to plants that are going into a garden where they are not going to receive regular watering; rather, they will be relying on natural rainfall and a little emergency irrigation from you if the weather is so dry that the plants are wilting. For those few prized plants that you want to keep growing at full throttle – such as your fast-growing annual vegetables – using a water-efficient irrigation system such as a wicking bed (see pages 79–95) will enable you to keep the plants growing without water stress, but also in a way that minimises water use.

When you buy a plant from a nursery, it has usually been grown under ideal conditions: it has been given virtually unlimited water and fertiliser to encourage it to grow as quickly as possible. The result of giving a plant maximum tender loving care with regard to water is that the pore spaces in the leaf (stomata) which regulate water loss tend to remain open most, if not all, of the time. This is fantastic if we need our plant to grow rapidly, and it helps the wholesale nursery grower who wants to get their plant to a saleable size as soon as possible.

However, this is not always the best thing for the unwitting gardener, who puts the plant into their garden and expects it to thrive even though it has usually been cut off from the unlimited water and fertiliser it has been receiving! We have seen plenty of situations over the years where gardeners have taken a plant home and put it straight into the ground without watering it in, and they have come back a week later to a water-stressed or dead plant. Angus remembers one gardener telling him that their dead plant was an Australian native species, which you are not supposed to water. (Boy, was the gardener wrong!)

The importance of acclimatising a plant that has been grown with unlimited water comes to the fore in the middle of summer, when the plant may face water stress and go downhill unless it can quickly establish roots in the soil into which it has been planted. The acclimatisation process enables the plant to become a lot more self-sufficient and capable of tapping into the subsoil's moisture reservoir.

How is it done?

In an ideal world, and if you have plenty of time on your hands, you can wean the plant off its diet of tender loving care before planting it out into the garden. By gradually reducing the amount of water it receives, you allow the plant to slow its growth and get used to more infrequent watering. Of course, this process can also be done after planting, but it is often much more difficult because the plant is likely to have sustained

These two-year-old Tasmanian blue gums (*Eucalyptus globulus*) have received no irrigation whatsoever since they were planted. They were established using the various techniques – such as acclimatisation and deep planting – outlined in this chapter.

some damage to its root system during the transplanting operation.

If the plant was being watered every day (which is usually what happens at a nursery), then cut the watering back to every second day. When it is clear that the plant is coping with this, then the watering regime can be reduced even further. Look at the growing tips of the plant to see how the plant is coping. Continual soft, sappy new growth is a sign that the plant is growing to its full potential. When the growing tips stop producing soft new growth, then the plant is 'hardening up' to the point where reducing the water supply is not going to do any long-term damage; rather, the plant will adjust its growth rate to a level that is sustainable with little to no additional irrigation.

Having said all this, we want to again emphasise that there will be situations where we will want to continue the tender loving care of supplying a particular plant with unlimited water and nutrients. In particular, fast-growing fruits and vegetables or prized ornamental feature plants (such as roses or dahlias) will benefit enormously from a stress-free environment in order to reach their full productive potential.

AVOIDING TRANSPLANT SHOCK

When you plant a pot plant into your garden, the root system has to learn to live in soil rather than potting mix. Modern potting mixes rarely if ever contain soil, or any mineral ingredients for that matter (not even sand). Most are now made mainly from composted pine bark and coir (coconut) fibre, as these ingredients provide a sustainable, predictable, high-quality medium that encourages the maximum possible growth rate. Such mixes are well aerated, which allows roots to grow very quickly, thereby encouraging rapid growth above ground level as well. By using a more open potting mix, wholesale nurseries are able to grow their plants to a saleable size in the minimum possible time, and thus be more profitable.

While these modern potting mixes do deliver extraordinary growth rates, they have also created a problem for the gardener who is

APPLYING ANTITRANSPIRANTS

A rapid way to acclimatise your plants to less water is to apply substances known as antitranspirants. The main way that plants lose water from their foliage is via the stomata, the tiny vents that are found all over the leaf surface. When water is available, the stomata open up and allow the transfer of gases and water vapour, which in turn creates the opportunity for plant growth. When moisture is scarce, the stomata close to preserve the dwindling water supply within the plant, a bit like turning off a tap.

We can mimic the effect of the plant closing its stomata by spraying both the upper and lower leaf surfaces with antitranspirants. There are various brand names for these products – such as WiltNot, DroughtShield and Envy – but essentially they are all water-emulsifiable polymer concentrates that form a semi-permeable, biodegradable film on the leaf surface that acts as a temporary check on water loss. This is particularly useful when you are transplanting or when plants are likely to be water-stressed. Antitranspirants can also protect the leaves from frost damage.

trying to establish the plant in their garden, particularly in a heavy clay soil. In effect, the pot plant is thrown into a situation where the fast-growing roots meet a wall of solid clay, and they can struggle to establish. Heavy rain can cause waterlogging of clay soils, leading to root rot and possible death of the newly planted pot plant. The answer to this problem is to dig wide and deep when you prepare your planting hole, and dig some potting mix or well rotted manure or compost through the soil that you will use to backfill the hole – the more the merrier! It is also advisable not to put too much organic matter in the bottom of the planting hole, because if there is a lot of water in the bottom of the hole – particularly in a heavy clay soil – the soil can become waterlogged, which creates an oxygen-depleted environment that is unfavourable for root establishment.

Digging so-called clay breakers into the soil at the base of your planting hole is another simple thing you can do to improve the conditions for the establishment of new root systems. Gypsum is relatively inexpensive, and to start with it can be applied at a rate of a couple of large handfuls per square metre (see page 101 for more information on gypsum).

The most important thing to remember when it comes to changing your plant from potting mix to garden soil is to use your common sense. Imagine the tiny feeder roots of your new plant trying to grow into the garden soil. If it is a solid mass that you find hard to dig, then your plant's roots will also find it difficult to penetrate the soil. A handy test is to try to push a screwdriver into the soil that you are hoping the roots will grow into. If you are finding the soil difficult to penetrate, then imagine how hard it will be for the plant's roots! Turning over the soil is the easiest and simplest way to provide a well-aerated root environment. However, in the long-term we want the soil around the roots to remain loose and friable after the planting hole has been filled, and this is where clay breakers are particularly useful.

Turning over the soil is the easiest and simplest way to provide a well-aerated root environment.

Left: Loosening the soil at the base of the planting hole greatly assists with root growth deep into the earth.

A well-prepared planting hole will ensure that plant roots establish quickly into the surrounding soil, enabling the plant to find its own water.

Maximum saturation

One of the simplest ways to improve your plant's chances of survival is to make sure it has its own little reservoir of water in its root ball **before** you plant it in the ground. By immersing the plant in an appropriate solution of water and root-inducing substances before planting, you will ensure that the entire root ball is storing as much water (and as many nutrients) as possible to keep the plant alive while the roots start to extend into their new soil home and find whatever stored moisture is available in the surrounding soil profile.

We find that the best way to prepare for transplanting is to soak the plant while it is still in its pot. Place the pot into a container of water mixed with an appropriate organic additive that fertilises the plant and provides growth regulators. This will enhance the new root growth that needs to happen as soon as possible after planting. We prefer to use 'worm juice', which is diluted leachate from our worm farms, as it provides not only nutrients but also

a host of beneficial microbes that proliferate in the worm farm. If you can't generate your own liquid preparation, there are many readily available liquid organic preparations (such as GOGO Juice from Australian manufacturer Neutrog). Using a fresh liquid preparation, however, ensures that your plant receives the maximum biological benefits.

It is also important to ensure (if at all possible) that the planting hole itself is fully charged with moisture just before planting. If the soil is naturally wet, or there has been good recent rainfall, then you don't need to add water at planting time. However, if your soil is dry, then it will tend to suck water away from the moist root ball by capillary action, as the water wants to move from moist soil particles to dry ones. Another possibility at this stage is to apply a liquid gypsum product along with the irrigation water you are using to wet the planting hole, as this will help to loosen the soil and therefore make it easier for the plant's roots to expand outwards to access the reservoir of water stored in the surrounding soil.

Above left: Thoroughly wetting the planting hole greatly improves the success rate of new plantings.

Above right: If there is a possibility of root damage during the transplanting process, then it is a good idea to reduce the amount of soft new foliage growth to lessen the plant's water demands while new roots establish in the soil.

As well as soaking the planting hole before planting, a thorough soaking of the planting area once your plant has gone into the ground and you have backfilled the hole will further help to ensure that the moisture level within the root ball is the same as that outside it, and that immediate water stress will not be a problem for your newly transplanted botanical treasure. Soaking the planting area after planting will also encourage the soil particles to make good contact with the roots, which in turn helps to facilitate the transfer of water from soil particles to the root system.

Reduce the plant's foliage

At planting time, we need to 'guesstimate' how much of the root system will survive and become functional in its new home. It is very difficult to completely avoid damaging the root system of a plant, even when it is coming out of a pot – and we can be certain of damage if a plant has been dug up from the ground for transplanting. If the root system of the plant is damaged in any way, then it is a good idea to reduce the number of leaves proportionate to the root loss (for example, if half of the roots are damaged, then remove half of the leaves). Even if the root system is not damaged, there is still a case for pruning the top of the plant back (especially if you know that the plant will be subject to dry periods, such as a roadside tree).

It is also important to assess whether all of the foliage on your potted plant is going to survive transplantation to a potentially drier environment, because the plant has a limited reservoir of water to call upon. Your potted plant fresh from the nursery will continue to grow thanks to the controlled-release fertiliser incorporated into the potting mix that ends up in the planting hole. If there is too much foliage relative to the size of the root ball, then it may wilt easily. Reducing the amount of foliage may be the best thing for the plant.

Balancing the foliage volume and the root volume is particularly important whenever you are transplanting plants around your garden. Any transplanting process is potentially damaging to the root system, so do not be timid when it comes to pruning back the leaves of a plant that is about to be transplanted. The larger a plant is,

Deep planting involves burying some of the stem to encourage more roots to grow.

the harder it will be to retain the entire root ball intact, and so the more foliage needs to be removed to create a new temporary balance between the damaged root system (and therefore its reduced capacity to take up water) and the amount of foliage on the plant that is transpiring moisture to the atmosphere. In the home garden, it is often the case that a large shrub or tree needs to be moved – sometimes at short notice – and we usually have to rely on hand tools or small digging machines, whereas wholesale tree nurseries have specialised equipment that enables them to dig up large established trees with minimal damage to the root system.

DEEP PLANTING

Every so often you come across something that challenges conventional wisdom and is therefore easily dismissed, but when you actually give it a try, it works! Such has been the case for us with the concept of deep planting, particularly with woody plants (for example, shrubs and trees). Just about every gardening book follows the standard planting advice as far as planting depth goes: the plant should end up being put in the ground at the same depth as it was in its pot, because burying the stem (as we are advocating in certain situations) would cause it to rot and the plant to die. But deep planting involves burying some of the stem to encourage more roots to grow.

Having road-tested the idea of deep planting on dozens of different species, Angus is firmly convinced that the traditional wisdom needs to be amended to acknowledge the profound advantages that deep planting brings to a wide variety of horticultural situations. The incredible success of this technique in improving the survival and subsequent growth of trees and shrubs can be used as a potent method for fighting climate change, as it is absolutely certain that this is a guaranteed way of absorbing carbon from our

TO ROOT PRUNE OR NOT TO ROOT PRUNE?

Root pruning is a somewhat controversial subject. In our experience, if a plant is root-bound, then it will benefit from the pruning of affected roots to encourage a downward- and outward-growing root system. By 'root-bound', we mean that a plant's root system has been constrained within a pot for so long that it is growing at odd angles or in a circle (see the photo above, where the main root is growing in a tight spiral). As the plant grows, it will effectively 'strangle' itself; it will never grow to its full potential and is likely to blow over in a strong windstorm. As the minimum preparation before planting, tease out any twisted roots and pinch off any that will not fit comfortably into the planting hole. You may need to use secateurs or a knife to perform more drastic surgery if the plant is severely root-bound, and you will also need to prune some of the foliage in this situation.

atmosphere and sequestering it in the woody tissues of trees and shrub for the long term.

Angus was initially alerted to the idea of deep planting by an environmentalist, the late Bill Hicks, who played an active role in Landcare projects in the upper Hunter Valley of New South Wales. Bill was particularly interested in the revegetation and stabilisation of river and creek banks that had previously been revegetated using the weeping willow (*Salix babylonica*), a deciduous exotic tree that was introduced to Australia early on by European settlers no doubt because it is so easy to propagate. While the weeping willow grows well alongside watercourses, as it loves the extra water, its falling autumn leaves end up in the water where they decompose and rob the water of oxygen – and this is disastrous for the ecology of the waterway. One of the consequences has been a tragic loss of biodiversity among species of freshwater fish.

Evergreen Australian species such as wattles (*Acacia* species) and eucalypts do not drop their leaves each year, but were traditionally seen as unsuitable for revegetation works because, when planted using conventional techniques and planting depths, they tended to simply wash away in the next flood. The willow trees that had been established by planting cuttings of long, leafless stems had a much deeper and therefore more secure root system that did not wash away. Bill wondered whether indigenous species could be planted deeper to emulate the success of the exotic willow trees. His deep-planted eucalypts and wattles were an overwhelming success: not only did they survive, but their growth rates were spectacular compared to those of the same species planted at the conventional depth.

Try it yourself at home

Why is deep planting so useful for the gardener? Because burying part of the stem usually causes new roots to form on the buried part of the stem, it means that as the plant establishes it has the potential to develop a much bigger and deeper root system than if it had been planted at a normal depth. Having a whole extra root system established in the deeper layers of soil gives the plant access to a much greater reservoir of water and nutrients.

Other advantages of deep planting include a more resilient plant, as the original root system that the plant had in its pot has been planted much deeper than normal and hopefully into subsoil that contains extra moisture at most times of the year. Deep planting also means that the plant is better able to withstand wind damage (so staking is not necessary) and predation from rabbits, kangaroos, wallabies and so on. Planting more deeply than usual can be especially important if the plant is root-bound in its pot. In our experience, plants that look like they are ready for the local nursery's specials table thrive when deep planted, as the new root system that develops is healthier and able to grow unhindered.

Leggy seedlings – such as annual flowers and vegetables in punnets – should also be planted as deep as possible. This stabilises them and stops them from falling over while the roots are establishing in their new home (of course, it is much better to have seedlings that are not leggy, but sometimes we have no choice).

LONG AND LEGGY

Bill Hicks was an unsung horticultural innovator, and his greatest gift of all was a specialist technique he called 'long-stem planting'. Bill's concept was to deliberately encourage young saplings in special containers called forestry tubes to form extra-long, leggy stems up to a metre in height that could then be planted extra deep to ensure they had the best chance to stabilise the waterways he was seeking to revegetate. The plants are given extra controlled-release fertiliser, and the tubes are held relatively close together so competition for light also encourages extra-long stems. This is a technique that can be easily emulated in the home garden.

Above left and right: These Tasmanian blue gums (*Eucalyptus globulus*) were deep planted on Angus's farm. The photo on the left was taken in spring 2021, and the one on the right shows the same trees at the end of summer. The trees had roughly doubled in height in just a few months.

Deep planting

Provided your soil has reasonable drainage and is not too rocky, it is well worth experimenting with deep planting in your own garden. Here is the method Angus uses on the farm when establishing trees and shrubs.

Step 1 Dig a hole as deep as your soil will allow. Be careful with drill-mounted augers, as they can whiplash back and hurt you if you hit an obstruction such as a rock, a tree root or heavy clay subsoil. Hand-held augers are a safer alternative if you are inexperienced with the drill-mounted kind.

Step 2 Thoroughly wet the hole by pouring at least a litre of water into it.

Step 3 After removing the foliage from the base of the stem (which will end up below soil level), submerge the root ball in a bucket of water while still in its pot to ensure that it is thoroughly saturated before planting.

Step 4 Lower the defoliated stem and saturated root ball into the planting hole.

Step 5 When the plant is in place, the hole is ready to be backfilled. This shows you how deep the plant is in the ground.

Step 6 Angus mixes biochar and worm castings with the excavated topsoil to create the best possible medium to use for backfilling the planting hole.

Steps continued >

Step 1

Step 4

Step 2

Step 3

Step 5

Step 6

Step 7 Carefully backfill the planting hole with the mix of topsoil, worm castings and biochar for optimum establishment of the tree, and water in the plant.

Left: We dug up one of our deep-planted Tasmanian blue gums (*Eucalyptus globulus*) to illustrate the results with the root development. Note the very long taproot, as well as the numerous lateral roots that have developed from the buried part of the stem.

DEEP WATERING

The establishment of your plants in the soil is the next phase of creating a futureproof garden, and this is particularly important with woody plants because they are so long-lived. Clearly, the larger the plant, the bigger the root system needs to be to service its water requirements; however, it is the distribution of this root system within the soil profile that is the critical issue.

If water only penetrates the topsoil and never soaks any deeper, the plant will produce most, if not all, of its roots in that moist upper zone. On the other hand, if we ensure that the subsoil is kept as moist as possible, then there is the opportunity to train the root systems of our plants to grow downwards and search for water in those moist lower layers of soil.

There are three ways to encourage the roots of your plants to grow down into the subsoil:

1 **deep planting** (see pages 153–9)

2 **creating an artificial dam around the base of the plant** – you can use some of the soil that is left over from digging the planting hole to create a little water-holding moat around the base of the plant. This will retain any moisture that comes as either rainfall or irrigation.

3 **water-efficient irrigation techniques** – this ensures that most of the water is channelled downwards to the subsoil each time you irrigate. Avoid irrigation methods that cause a lot of water loss from evaporation, such as overhead sprinklers. The many and varied options when it comes to irrigation systems are covered in detail in Chapter 3.

It is the distribution of the root system within the soil profile that is the critical issue.

OVERCOMING HYDROPHOBIC SOILS

The very top layer of your soil is particularly prone to becoming **hydrophobic** (moisture repelling). This layer is constantly in contact with fresh and rotting organic matter, which sometimes coats the soil particles and makes them hard to wet. One way to solve this problem is by inverting the top layer of your soil, thereby bringing non-hydrophobic particles up to the surface and distributing the hydrophobic particles in the lower layers of soil, where they will gradually lose that unwanted property.

One of the time-honoured practices within vegetable gardening is to dig the garden over when preparing for a new crop. There are various methods that you can use, but one of the simplest and easiest is to completely invert the topsoil. First, remove a spadeful of topsoil, and set it aside. Next, dig up a spadeful of topsoil from beside the first hole, turn it upside down and place it into the first hole. Keep going along the row until the whole area of soil has been inverted (the last hole is filled with the upside down topsoil from the first hole). It is particularly important to do this digging when the soil is neither wet nor dry (just moist), as this helps the clods of soil

hang together better and ensures that your soil has a better structure, which in turn gives you a better balance between aeration and moisture in your soil. If you are working on a larger scale, you may want to hire a specialist plough called a mouldboard that completely inverts the furrow of soil it creates as it moves along a row.

As you turn over your soil in the home garden, you also need to break up any especially large clods; you are aiming for an ideal structure of predominantly small soil particles (crumbs). These crumbs should be a few millimetres to a few centimetres in diameter, so it is easy for plant roots to grow between the crumbs but they can still suck out the moisture that is stored in the crumbs.

Mulching (see pages 118–21) can also overcome hydrophobic soil problems by creating a surface that water can easily penetrate, and by holding the water in place while it gradually percolates down through the soil. Another approach is to use **soil-wetting agents** (see page 62) that are specially formulated for this problem. They can be applied either as liquids that are watered or sprayed onto the soil surface, or as solids that are dug into the topsoil – this is a useful approach if the soil is also showing signs of compaction, something that will further limit its capacity to absorb moisture.

Far left: Hydrophobic soils repel liquid, making it difficult for water to infiltrate the topsoil.

Left: Sugar-cane residue is one of the many materials that can be used as mulch to help overcome the dire problem of hydrophobic soils.

7

WATER-EFFICIENT PLANTS

Climate change is linked to temperature increases, rainfall fluctuations (both flood and drought) and a surge in severe weather events, such as cyclones and hailstorms. We need to adapt our garden designs by selecting plants that will cope with these extremes.

The following directory profiles 200 native and exotic plants that are particularly tolerant of dry conditions. Many can also cope with – and often thrive in – an overabundance of moisture. There are many beautiful ornamental plants, as well as a wealth of water-efficient alternatives to traditional edible plants. Most of them feature adaptations such as leathery or spiky leaves that maximise the plant's efficient use of water, or resilient root systems that can survive either very dry or very wet conditions.

Within the Native Plants directory, we highlight the Australian plants that boast delightful flowers and/or foliage. There is a focus on plants that create useful food sources and habitats for Australian animals and insects.

We also point out tasty Australian bush foods – such as muntries (*Kunzea pomifera*) and warrigal greens (*Tetragonia tetragonioides*) – that can be grown in the garden with minimal water. In general, however, to reach their full productive potential, plants grown for food may require extra water in dry conditions, as it is necessary for the production of abundant leaves, flowers and fruits. In these cases, using a wicking bed or another similar system is the ideal way to ensure the best water efficiency.

In the Exotic Plants directory, you'll find many appealing cacti, succulents and other plants that have adapted over time to withstand dry periods and regions. They include garden favourites such as English lavender (*Lavandula angustifolia*) and

Chinese wisteria (*Wisteria sinensis*), as well as herbs, fruits and vegetables.

By combining our list of water-efficient plants with the various strategies for futureproofing your garden detailed throughout the book, you can create a sustainable, attractive and productive garden wherever you live.

A GUIDE TO THE WATER-DROP SYMBOL

The water needs of each plant are given with a water-drop rating that ranges from one to three drops, and we'd like to explain that in more depth.

Many plants on the list have been allocated one water drop; however, this doesn't mean they can be neglected entirely. Firstly, any plants grown in pots will need more water than usual, because they don't have any extra reservoirs to draw on – and that includes all of the one-drop plants. Secondly, all plants need extra water in the establishment phase, so even the most drought-tolerant plant on the list will require more water while it is becoming established (regardless of whether this is in a pot or in the ground).

Wicking beds and drip irrigation are great for edible plants and any other species that require a period of additional water. Plants that have been given a rating of two or three water drops are perfect candidates for wicking beds, which will provide their extra water needs in a sustainable way.

PLANT LIST SYMBOLS

The plant entries on the following pages include a range of symbols that provide at-a-glance information about each plant.

C	Tolerates coastal conditions		Red flower colour	AY	Flowers all year
D	Drought-tolerant		Orange flower colour	SpS	Flowers in two seasons
D+W	Tolerates both dry and wet conditions		Yellow flower colour	S-W	Flowers in three seasons
E	Edible		Green flower colour		Attracts birds
F	Fire retardant		Blue flower colour		Attracts butterflies
S	Salt-tolerant		Mauve flower colour		Attracts bees
W	Prefers wet conditions		Purple flower colour		Attracts other insects
↑	Height		Pink flower colour		Attracts lizards
↔	Width		Brown flower colour		Attracts bats
	Tolerates shade		White flower colour		Attracts frogs
	Tolerates part-shade		Cream flower colour		Attracts possums
	Tolerates light shade	I	Insignificant flowers	1	Low water needs
	Tolerates full sun		Multiple flower colours	2	Medium water needs
	No frost tolerance		Bicolour flowers	3	High water needs
L	Low frost tolerance	Sp	Flowers in spring		*Plants grown in pots may need more water*
M	Medium frost tolerance	S	Flowers in summer		
H	High frost tolerance	A	Flowers in autumn		
		W	Flowers in winter		

NATIVE PLANTS

1. *Acacia aphylla* (leafless rock wattle)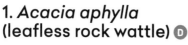

An outstanding drought-tolerant plant because of its leafless form, this wattle also provides shelter for small creatures because of its spiny branches. It is native to the area around Perth, and it needs a very well-drained soil and a good amount of sun. The sharp branches create an interesting effect, making it a great plant for landscaping or architectural projects, or just for those looking for a unique, low-maintenance shrub for dry areas. **Climate:** Arid, semi-arid. **Soil:** Well-drained; loamy or sandy, poor soil.

2. *Acacia cardiophylla* (Wyalong wattle)

This wattle has quite a compact, shrubby growth habit, making it useful for a range of garden sizes, provided it gets full sun. It has grey-green feathery foliage and in spring puts on a wonderful display of globular bright yellow flowers that have a soft scent of nectar. The height varies from low and bushy to quite tall, making it useful as a screen or as a feature plant for its vibrant display and lovely foliage. **Climate:** Cool, cool to warm temperate, Mediterranean. **Soil:** Well-drained; loamy or sandy.

3. *Acacia cognata* 'Burgundy Cascade'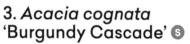

A beautiful landscaping and screening plant, 'Burgundy Cascade' has fine, green, weeping leaves with burgundy edges, creating a display of softly contrasting colour in the garden. It is grown primarily for its foliage, which provides a great display all through the year. The dense growth habit and fast growth rate make it perfect for screening, or it can also make a great feature plant with its sculptural weeping form. **Climate:** Cool to warm temperate, Mediterranean. **Soil:** Moderate to well-drained; loamy or sandy.

4. *Acacia cognata* 'Lime Magik'

'Lime Magik' is a fabulous screening plant with soft, willowy foliage in a vibrant lime colour. Forming a large shrub or small tree, it is a great plant for filling out the garden with swathes of colour, and it doesn't require much maintenance at all – just a light pruning to get it into the shape you want. While it can get up to 10 metres high, pruning it will keep it in a more compact shape. The width of the plant is about 2–3 metres, so it is ideal to fill medium to large spaces in the garden or landscape. **Climate:** Cool, cool to warm temperate, Mediterranean. **Soil:** Well-drained; clayey, loamy or sandy.

5. *Acacia cultriformis* 'Cascade'

A spectacular plant, it can be used for a striking display of cascading foliage or as a dense ground cover. Plant it in a tall planter box or on top of a wall or bank so the foliage can spill out vertically, forming a curtain of silvery green with clusters of bright golden flowers appearing in spring. The dense foliage is perfect for attracting small birds such as wrens to the garden, as they dart around searching for insects in the thicket. **Climate:** Cool, cool to warm temperate, Mediterranean. **Soil:** Moderate to well-drained; loamy or sandy, potting mix.

6. *Acacia glaucoptera* (clay wattle)

This beautiful and unusual wattle has distinctive and interesting foliage, with deep red new growth, plus bright ball-shaped flowers that appear to grow straight from the leaves. Growing to a medium-sized shrub with a spreading habit, it makes a great addition to any native garden for its unique features. It is tolerant of moderate to heavy frosts, and it will thrive best in a part-shade position, but can tolerate dappled shade and full sun as well. Prune regularly to stimulate the gorgeous red new growth and maintain shape. **Climate:** Cool, cool to warm temperate, Mediterranean, semi-arid. **Soil:** Well-drained; clayey, loamy or sandy.

7. *Acacia iteaphylla* (Flinders Ranges wattle)

This is a beautiful ornamental wattle with weeping foliage and bursts of pale yellow flowers in spring. After flowering, the young seed pods also provide a lovely display with their silvery tones. An adaptable plant, it will grow to a medium or large shrub and forms a dense thicket, making it great for screening and windbreaks. **Climate:** Cool, cool temperate, Mediterranean. **Soil:** Well-drained; clayey, loamy or sandy, potting mix.

8. *Acacia lineata* (streaked wattle)

A wonderful and adaptable wattle, this is a great shrub for challenging conditions as it is very drought- and frost-tolerant, being native to dry forest and scrub throughout central New South Wales. It is also a fantastic ornamental plant, growing into a dense shrub and bursting into a spectacular show of golden flowers in spring. The thick and bushy habit makes this wattle a great shelter and habitat for small birds, and it works well as a windbreak to protect other plants. **Climate:** Cool, cool temperate, Mediterranean. **Soil:** Well-drained; loamy or sandy.

9. *Acacia littorea* (shark tooth wattle)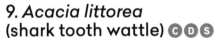

Named for its small triangular leaves, this is a stunning wattle when in bloom, well worth growing for the impressive show of spring flowers. It is a dense shrub with aromatic leaves, perfect for coastal gardens as it naturally grows in sandy soils. A full-sun position and well-drained soil are best for this plant, and it is tolerant of drought and light frosts. **Climate:** Warm temperate, Mediterranean. **Soil:** Well-drained; loamy or sandy, saline soil.

10. *Acacia merinthophora* (zigzag wattle)

A graceful wattle species from Western Australia, this plant also does well on the east coast. It is a lovely ornamental plant, making a great addition to the garden for its attractive weeping form and large golden flowers. The intricate branches make beautiful additions to floral arrangements as well. Flowering from early winter to early spring, the stout yellow flowers stand out against the long thin leaf stalks. Grow in a well-drained soil that is light to medium in texture, and position in full sun for best results, though it will tolerate light shade. **Climate:** Cool to warm temperate, Mediterranean. **Soil:** Well-drained; loamy or sandy.

11. *Acacia pravissima* 'Bushwalk Baby'

A low ground cover with beautiful foliage, this can be grown to trail over walls or hanging containers. Small, yellow, globular flowers appear in spring, and pruning after flowering will help to maintain a neat shape. This is a great ornamental plant for container gardening and courtyards, as long as there is good sunlight. **Climate:** Cool to warm temperate, Mediterranean. **Soil:** Well-drained; clayey, loamy or sandy, potting mix.

12. *Actinotus helianthi* (flannel flower)

The soft white flannel flower is a classic Australian wildflower and a wonderful addition to the garden, as well as making a lovely cut flower. It is a great plant to grow in pots, because it needs very free-draining sandy soil that can be difficult to create in a garden bed. The foliage is pale green with a downy texture, and the characteristic white flowers with green petal tips appear gradually, peaking in spring and summer. Cutting the flowers for vases or bouquets will help to prune the plant and encourage more flowers the following season. **Climate:** Cool to warm temperate, Mediterranean. **Soil:** Well-drained; loamy or sandy, potting mix.

13. *Adenanthos cuneatus* 'Coral Carpet'

0.2–0.3 m

1.5–2 m

A great foliage plant for year-round colour, this ground cover can be used to bring vibrant red tones to a patch of the garden or to spill out from a container. The bright red new growth is the outstanding feature of the plant, although the little red flowers will also attract small nectar-eating birds to the garden. It is best grown in full sun, as this will give the new growth a deeper colour. Originating from coastal areas of Western Australia, it will do best in similar climates in southern Australia. **Climate:** Cool to warm temperate, Mediterranean. **Soil:** Well-drained; loamy or sandy.

14. *Adenanthos cuneatus* 'Flat Out'

0.1–0.3 m

0.75–1 m

This ground cover has beautiful deep red-bronze new growth and a prostrate form perfect for cascading down embankments or planting in rockeries. It can also be grown in containers. While the ornamental foliage and low spreading habit are the main features of this plant, it also produces small red flowers in spring and summer that attract nectar-eating birds to the garden. Grow in a part-shade to full-sun position, and trim every so often to remove any dead or lacklustre branches. **Climate:** Cool to warm temperate, Mediterranean, semi-arid. **Soil:** Well-drained; clayey, loamy or sandy.

15. *Adenanthos sericeus* 'Compact'

1 m

1 m

This dwarf cultivar of the woolly bush has distinctive silver-tinged foliage. Great for landscaping and tactile gardens, it features small red flowers in spring. Grow it in a well-drained soil, and it works well in containers and raised beds. It is tolerant of dry periods once established and is a great low-maintenance plant generally. The naturally compact shape means that it hardly ever needs pruning. **Climate:** Cool to warm temperate, Mediterranean, semi-arid. **Soil:** Well-drained; clayey, loamy or sandy.

16. *Agonis flexuosa* 'Burgundy'

3–6 m

2–4 m

This cultivar of the willow peppermint has beautiful deep burgundy new growth that looks striking in the garden. It can be planted as a screen or a feature plant, with the unique foliage contrasting well with other plants. Older leaves are a soft green, so the plant creates a wash of green and burgundy shades throughout the year. It is a good plant for coastal gardens and can be pruned to the shape desired. Apply some native fertiliser in spring and summer to keep it looking its best. **Climate:** Cool, cool to warm temperate, Mediterranean, subtropical. **Soil:** Well-drained; clayey, loamy or sandy, potting mix.

17. *Allocasuarina grampiana* (Grampians sheoak)

1–4 m

1.5–2 m

A rare large shrub or small tree endemic to the Grampians in Victoria, this sheoak has attractive blue-grey foliage and would make a great native alternative to exotic conifers in the garden. Like many plants in this family, it produces male and female flowers on different plants. The female ones are deep red and have many styles, giving them a fluffy appearance. The branchlets are coated in a waxy bloom, giving the foliage its soft blue colour, and the waxy coating also helps to make this a wonderfully drought-tolerant plant. **Climate:** Cool, cool to warm temperate, Mediterranean, semi-arid. **Soil:** Well-drained; loamy or sandy.

18. *Alyogyne* 'Blue Heeler'

0.3–0.5 m

0.5–1 m

This form of the native hibiscus is a ground cover, growing to less than half a metre in height and just a metre in width. It has purple hibiscus flowers throughout the warmer months. It works well in the foreground of mixed plantings or in rockeries, and can be grown in a container in a smaller garden provided it gets enough sun. Prune lightly after flowering. **Climate:** Cool to warm temperate, Mediterranean, subtropical. **Soil:** Well-drained; clayey, loamy or sandy.

19. *Alyogyne hakeifolia* (native hibiscus)

2–3 m
1.5–2 m

Native hibiscus has outstanding large flowers, and comes in yellow, pink or mauve forms. The fine needle-like leaves help this plant to withstand dry conditions in its native habitat in south-eastern Western Australia and South Australia. It will grow best in areas with low humidity, and it needs a well-drained soil in full sun. Flowers appear in summer and autumn, putting on an impressive display. **Climate:** Cool to warm temperate, Mediterranean, semi-arid. **Soil:** Well-drained; loamy or sandy.

20. *Alyogyne huegelii* 'Karana'

1–1.5 m
1–1.5 m

A new cultivar of the native hibiscus, 'Karana' looks great planted with either natives or exotics. It has abundant mauve-coloured flowers from spring to autumn, and a dense growth habit. Growing to around 1.5 metres tall and wide, it is relatively compact and responds well to light pruning. It should be pruned after flowering, and can be trimmed at other times to the desired shape. **Climate:** Cool to warm temperate, Mediterranean, semi-arid, subtropical. **Soil:** Well-drained; clayey, loamy or sandy.

21. *Anigozanthos flavidus* 'Landscape Lilac'

0.5–2 m
0.5–1 m

From the Tall and Tough range by Gardening With Angus, this kangaroo paw has striking flowers that sit well above the foliage. The flower colour changes as the buds open, from pale purple to deeper purple, and the flowers have bright orange stamens. Plant in full sun for best flowering – the more sun it gets, the better it will flower. It can be pruned to remove old or damaged foliage, and should be cut right back once it has finished flowering, removing the old flower stems. **Climate:** Cool to warm temperate, Mediterranean, subtropical. **Soil:** Moist to well-drained, dry; clayey, loamy or sandy.

22. *Apium insulare* (Flinders Island celery)

0.5–1 m
0.3–0.5 m

This tough edible plant is related to the vegetable celery, and the stems can be used to replace celery in meals. The leaves can also be used in the same way as parsley. It is a hardy coastal plant that will grow in most types of soil, and it does best with consistent water and fertiliser. It can die down in winter but will resprout in warmer seasons, and it is also easy to grow from seed. **Climate:** Cool, cool to warm temperate, Mediterranean. **Soil:** Moist to well-drained; clayey, loamy or sandy, saline soil.

23. *Atriplex cinerea* (grey saltbush)

1–1.5 m
1 m

A tough and useful plant, grey saltbush is native to coastal areas in southern Australia. It grows in a range of soils, from sand dunes to coastal marshes, and it is excellent for stabilising soil prone to erosion. Grey saltbush copes well with harsh coastal conditions such as salt and winds. Growing to a small shrub, it has lovely silver foliage that can be eaten the same way as regular saltbush. It is an excellent perennial bush-food plant, and pruning will encourage more growth. **Climate:** Cool, cool to warm temperate, Mediterranean, semi-arid. **Soil:** Very well-drained; loamy or sandy, saline soil.

24. *Atriplex nummularia* (old man saltbush)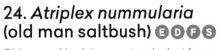

1–3 m
2–5 m

Old man saltbush is a very tough plant from arid inland areas of Australia; it is tolerant of high salinity, alkalinity and drought, and makes a good stock feed. It cannot tolerate high humidity levels or waterlogging, so it is best for dry climates. A sprawling woody shrub with ornamental silver foliage, the plant's leaves and seeds are edible. The fresh leaves can be fried and served with a variety of dishes. The South Australian Country Fire Service classifies it as a fire-retardant plant. **Climate:** Arid, cool, cool to warm temperate, Mediterranean, semi-arid, subtropical. **Soil:** Very well-drained; clayey, loamy or sandy, saline soil.

25. *Austromyrtus* 'Copper Tops'

This is one of the best bush-food plants, producing pretty white berries speckled with dark blue spots that give a purplish shade to the fruits. Developing in late summer and autumn, the berries have a sweet and tangy flavour, and they can be eaten fresh or used for jams and pies. Prune plants after harvesting to promote better fruiting the following season. Because of the plant's copper-tinged new growth, it is increasingly being used as a native (and edible) hedge, and it also grows well in pots and raised beds. **Climate:** Cool to warm temperate, Mediterranean, subtropical. **Soil:** Poor to well-drained; clayey, loamy or sandy.

26. *Backhousia citriodora* (lemon myrtle)

Lemon myrtle is both a beautiful tree and a tasty bush food that is becoming much more widely known and used. It can easily be grown as a shrub for smaller gardens, and the foliage harvested from pruning can be used for cooking and tea. Best grown in a sunny position, lemon myrtle needs a well-drained soil and some fertiliser and extra water in the warmer months to really flourish. The foliage is glossy and vibrant green, while the fluffy white flower clusters appear in summer and autumn and are quite striking. **Climate:** Cool to warm temperate, Mediterranean, subtropical. **Soil:** Poor to well-drained; clayey, loamy or sandy.

27. *Baeckea crassifolia* (desert heath myrtle)

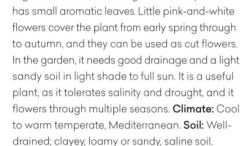

A great shrub for coastal gardens, this plant has small aromatic leaves. Little pink-and-white flowers cover the plant from early spring through to autumn, and they can be used as cut flowers. In the garden, it needs good drainage and a light sandy soil in light shade to full sun. It is a useful plant, as it tolerates salinity and drought, and it flowers through multiple seasons. **Climate:** Cool to warm temperate, Mediterranean. **Soil:** Well-drained; clayey, loamy or sandy, saline soil.

28. *Baeckea linifolia* (weeping baeckea)

An elegant weeping shrub with small white flowers, this is native to moist sites in eastern Victoria and New South Wales. It will tolerate drier soils as well, provided it has some shade and a good cover of mulch, but it does appreciate some extra water during dry times. Growing into a small to medium shrub, this plant is best placed somewhere you can enjoy the delicate flowers and the spicy scent of the leaves when they are crushed. It can also be used for cut flowers, as the flowers continue opening in the vase. **Climate:** Cool, cool to warm temperate, Mediterranean, subtropical. **Soil:** Well-drained; clayey, loamy or sandy.

29. *Banksia aemula* (wallum banksia)

The wallum banksia is a wonderful ornamental for any garden, with a sculptural gnarled appearance and yellow nectar-laden flowers that bring birds to the garden. It is native to coastal heath in New South Wales and Queensland. Perfect for growing in containers, it is low maintenance and can be pruned heavily, so you can shape it to any size to suit your space. It can be used as a feature plant for its architectural form, and it also makes a good screening plant. This banksia makes a great cut flower, too. **Climate:** Cool to warm temperate, Mediterranean, semi-arid, subtropical. **Soil:** Well-drained; clayey, loamy or sandy.

30. *Banksia baueri* (woolly banksia)

This banksia is a compact shrub with giant woolly flower heads that give it its common name. The stunning flowers are the main feature of this plant, and they can be cut and used for flower arrangements. It is a great plant for any garden, as it is low maintenance and can also be grown in large pots. Growing it in containers also helps to provide the best drainage, as this banksia needs a well-drained sandy soil. It requires full sun to both grow and flower well. **Climate:** Cool to warm temperate, Mediterranean. **Soil:** Well-drained; loamy or sandy.

31. *Banksia epica* (epic banksia)

The epic banksia makes a spectacular feature plant with its huge yellow flower heads and dense foliage, and the impressive blooms can also be used as cut flowers. A very low-maintenance plant for the garden, it can be hard to find in cultivation. It is well worth growing though, as it is rare in its native habitat in Western Australia, known from only two locations. It needs an extremely well-drained soil and full sun, and it is tolerant of drought and light frost once established. **Climate:** Cool to warm temperate, Mediterranean. **Soil:** Well-drained; clayey, loamy or sandy.

2–5 m
2–4 m
AY
1

32. *Banksia ericifolia* 'Little Eric'

An excellent banksia for hedging and screening, this small shrub also displays gorgeous orange flowers with maroon styles in winter and spring. The flowers attract nectar-eating birds and insects, making this a great plant for wildlife gardens. A very versatile plant, it is well-suited to coastal gardens and tolerates a range of soils. It is great for difficult spots, as it flowers even in part-shade and withstands dry soils. After flowering, it can be pruned to maintain a dense bushy form. **Climate:** Cool to warm temperate, Mediterranean, subtropical. **Soil:** Well-drained; loamy or sandy.

1.5–2 m
1–1.5 m
WSp
1

33. *Banksia* 'Giant Candles'

This banksia cultivar has outstanding dark orange flowers that can be up to 40 centimetres long, providing abundant nectar for wildlife in the garden throughout winter. The striking blooms can also be cut for flower arrangements, and they last well both on the plant and in the vase. An adaptable banksia for either coastal or inland gardens, it prefers a well-drained soil and needs full sun to flower at its best. It makes a great feature shrub or screen, and it can be pruned to maintain dense growth and a compact shape. **Climate:** Cool, cool to warm temperate, Mediterranean, subtropical. **Soil:** Well-drained; clayey, loamy or sandy.

3–4 m
2–2.5 m
WSp
1

34. *Banksia grandis* (bull banksia)

A stunning banksia from Western Australia, the bull banksia has very interesting toothed leaves and can be grown for that reason alone. The yellow flowers are very large, sometimes up to 40 centimetres in length, but it can take plants a long time to flower when grown from seed. It can be used as a cut flower, too. It makes a wonderful feature plant for both the foliage and flowers, and can be grown in a large container. Best suited to coastal areas with low humidity, it needs full sun and a well-drained soil. **Climate:** Cool to warm temperate, Mediterranean. **Soil:** Well-drained; clayey, loamy or sandy.

4–8 m
3–5 m
SpS
1

35. *Banksia integrifolia* 'Roller Coaster'

This cultivar has a very low cascading form, making it particularly good for growing on embankments or spilling out over a rockery or container. It is a fast-growing ground cover that can be used to stabilise sandy soils and banks. The leathery foliage is dark green with a silvery underside, and the yellow flowers begin to appear in autumn, providing an important source of nectar for wildlife. After flowering, the distinctive seed pods emerge, providing food for seed-eating birds such as the majestic yellow-tailed black cockatoo. **Climate:** Cool to warm temperate, Mediterranean. **Soil:** Well-drained; clayey, loamy or sandy.

0.1–0.15 m
4 m
AW
1

36. *Banksia menziesii* (Menzies' banksia)

An impressive ornamental, this banksia is often grown for cut flowers as it has large and showy flower heads in rusty red and orange. These gorgeous flowers will also attract nectar-eating birds to the garden. Growing to a large shrub or small tree, it can be used as a windbreak or screen in the garden. It needs a well-drained soil, and it can be hard to grow in areas with humid summers, such as the east coast, because it is prone to root rot. **Climate:** Cool, cool to warm temperate, Mediterranean, semi-arid. **Soil:** Well-drained; loamy or sandy.

5–10 m
5–10 m
AW
1

37. *Banksia occidentalis* (red swamp banksia)

2–7 m

2–5 m

A magnificent and highly ornamental shrub, the red swamp banksia is a great choice for the garden because of its attractive red-and-yellow flowers that appear sporadically throughout the year. Growing quickly into a large shrub or small tree, it makes a good windbreak or screen in the garden. It is native to swampy areas near the coast in Western Australia, but it is adaptable to other soils as well. Best suited to Mediterranean climates, it does not tolerate humid summers very well. **Climate:** Cool temperate, Mediterranean. **Soil:** Well-drained; loamy or sandy.

38. *Banksia petiolaris*

0.3–0.5 m

2–4 m

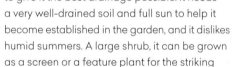
W–S

This is an interesting low-growing banksia that can be grown over an embankment, as a ground cover or in rockeries. As a spreading ground cover, it is a useful plant for controlling erosion. Vivid yellow flower spikes pop up from the foliage from winter to summer, making this a unique ornamental for the native garden. Happiest in a well-drained sandy soil and full sun, it can also be grown in light shade and will tolerate other soils as long as they are well-drained. It is also tolerant of alkaline soils. **Climate:** Cool, cool to warm temperate, Mediterranean, semi-arid. **Soil:** Well-drained; clayey, loamy or sandy.

39. *Banksia praemorsa* (cut-leaf banksia)

2–5 m
2–3 m

WSp

A medium shrub perfect for coastal gardens, the cut-leaf banksia is a lovely ornamental with prominent flowers in a dark red colour (or sometimes bright yellow). They can be used as cut flowers. Appearing in winter and spring, the flowers attract nectar-eating birds; the dense foliage provides a habitat for the birds. Native to Western Australia, this species can better withstand humid summers than other banksias from that state. **Climate:** Cool, cool to warm temperate, Mediterranean, semi-arid. **Soil:** Well-drained; clayey, loamy or sandy.

40. *Banksia prionotes* (orange banksia)

5–12 m
4–6 m

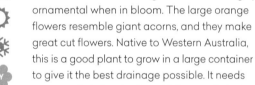

This banksia has stunning flowers and is highly ornamental when in bloom. The large orange flowers resemble giant acorns, and they make great cut flowers. Native to Western Australia, this is a good plant to grow in a large container to give it the best drainage possible. It needs a very well-drained soil and full sun to help it become established in the garden, and it dislikes humid summers. A large shrub, it can be grown as a screen or a feature plant for the striking flowers. **Climate:** Cool to warm temperate, Mediterranean, semi-arid. **Soil:** Well-drained; loamy or sandy.

41. *Banksia saxicola* (Grampians banksia)

3–6 m
3–4 m

SA

Ideal for cool climates, this banksia is native to the Grampians where it grows in exposed areas, making it a tough plant for the garden. It withstands frost and wind, and it can vary from a low shrub to a tree depending on how exposed it is to the elements. The shiny dark green foliage is one of the most attractive features of this plant, along with the yellow flowers and seed pods. Best grown in a well-drained soil, the Grampians banksia prefers a part-shade position in the garden, as it needs a cool root system. **Climate:** Cool, cool to warm temperate, Mediterranean. **Soil:** Well-drained; clayey, loamy or sandy.

42. *Banksia spinulosa* 'Birthday Candles'

0.4–0.5 m
0.5–1 m

AW

This cultivar grows into a compact bushy shrub, about half a metre high, with deep golden yellow flowers in autumn and winter. It is a useful plant that can be grown in containers to brighten up patios and small gardens, or planted en masse for a low-maintenance display. It needs a well-drained soil, and can be grown in raised beds or containers if your soil is too heavy. A tough plant, it can tolerate drought and windy conditions once established. Position in full sun for best flowering, and make sure to mulch well. **Climate:** Cool, cool to warm temperate, Mediterranean, subtropical. **Soil:** Well-drained; loamy or sandy.

43. *Beaufortia sparsa* (swamp bottlebrush)

1–3 m
1–2.5 m

The swamp bottlebrush is a spectacular shrub from Western Australia with orangey red bottlebrush flowers in spring and summer. It is a versatile ornamental, as it grows well in both dry and moist situations, making it perfect for difficult spots in the garden. A great feature of this plant is that it can be used as a cut flower; cutting the flowers will also prune the plant and encourage new growth. **Climate:** Cool to warm temperate, Mediterranean. **Soil:** Well-drained; loamy or sandy.

44. *Brachychiton rupestris* (Queensland bottle tree)

10–20 m
2–5 m

The Queensland bottle tree is a wonderful and adaptable feature plant for larger gardens, with its unique bottle-shaped trunk that can grow up to 2 metres in diameter. The bottle shape takes around five to eight years to develop. Endemic to a small area of central Queensland, it can be cultivated anywhere with a warm climate, and it is a drought-tolerant plant once established. It is deciduous, dropping its leaves before flowering in late spring and summer. This plant needs a well-drained soil and full sun. **Climate:** Warm temperate, Mediterranean, subtropical. **Soil:** Well-drained; loamy or sandy.

45. *Brachyscome multifida* 'Mauve Mystery'

0.1–0.2 m
0.2–0.3 m

This native daisy cultivar has interesting flowers that vary in shade from mauve to white, sometimes on the same flower, creating a beautiful display of mixed blooms all on the one plant. It is a very easy plant to grow and useful for a range of situations, from rockeries to hanging baskets. It is also a great plant for mass planting, because it flowers all year round and is low maintenance. It can be grown in most climates around Australia, provided it is protected from heavy frosts in cooler areas. **Climate:** Cool, cool to warm temperate, Mediterranean, subtropical. **Soil:** Moderate to well-drained; clayey, loamy or sandy.

46. *Brunonia australis* (blue pincushion)

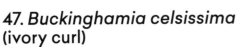

0.1–0.5 m
0.1–0.2 m

The distinctive flower heads of this perennial make it a beautiful ornamental for any garden, and particularly for cottage gardens. The delicate flower heads have many tiny flowers in pastel shades of blue, and they are borne on tall stems above the soft green foliage. Adaptable to most soils and climates, the plant does best in a well-drained soil in part-shade to full sun. It can sometimes grow more like an annual, but it can be propagated from seed easily. **Climate:** Cool, cool to warm temperate, Mediterranean, semi-arid, subtropical. **Soil:** Well-drained; clayey, loamy or sandy.

47. *Buckinghamia celsissima* (ivory curl)

7–25 m
1–4 m

A striking ornamental tree for medium to large gardens, the ivory curl puts on a marvellous display of long cream flowers in summer and autumn. The flowers cover the whole plant during flowering and are great for nectar-eating wildlife. The deep green foliage is also ornamental. Growing to a large tree in the wild, it is much smaller in cultivation and especially in cooler regions. Native to rainforest areas of Queensland, it is known to do well as far south as Melbourne. **Climate:** Warm temperate, subtropical. **Soil:** Well-drained; clayey, loamy or sandy.

48. *Bulbine bulbosa* (bulbine lily)

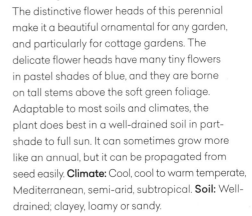

0.5–0.8 m
0.3–0.5 m

This is a beautiful native for flower gardens, with bright yellow flowers and strappy leaves. The flowers have a light scent and appear from spring through to autumn, and the plant is a great alternative to exotic bulbs. It grows in a range of soils across Australia, and it is tolerant of light frost and dry conditions. As it grows from a corm, it can die down during drought conditions and regrow when water is available – a great adaptation to water stress. The corm is also edible; large ones should be roasted for the best flavour. **Climate:** Cool, cool to warm temperate, Mediterranean, subtropical. **Soil:** Well-drained; loamy or sandy.

1.5–4 m

1.5–3 m

49. *Bursaria spinosa* (sweet bursaria)

Ranging from a small shrub to a small tree in form, this is a beautiful native for the flower garden as it produces masses of scented white flowers in summer. The tiny flowers grow in dense clusters, covering the plant in fluffy white drifts. Both the fragrant flowers and the spiky foliage are great for wildlife, and the flowers also attract butterflies. It is a very low-maintenance plant that just needs a yearly prune to keep it tidy. **Climate:** Cool to warm temperate, Mediterranean, subtropical. **Soil:** Moist to well-drained; clayey, loamy or sandy.

0.1–0.3 m

0.3 m

50. *Calandrinia balonensis* (parakeelya) D E

Parakeelya is a drought-tolerant ornamental and bush-food plant. The roots and leaves are edible, as well as the seeds. It is in the purslane family and is actually a succulent, though the leaves are softer and darker green than most succulents. Growing as a prostrate herb, it has bright pink flowers in spring and summer. Native to arid regions, it needs very good drainage and will thrive in a dry and sunny spot. It can be grown in containers and hanging baskets in humid areas. It is an annual or biennial and will self-sow in the garden. **Climate:** Cool to warm temperate, Mediterranean, semi-arid, subtropical. **Soil:** Well-drained; loamy or sandy.

2–2.5 m
1–1.5 m

51. *Callistemon* 'All Aglow'

This is a striking bottlebrush that has beautifully coloured new growth as well as bright reddish pink flowers in abundance. Perfect for small gardens, it has a compact shape and can be pruned as much as required. It is a wonderful hedging plant because of the colourful new growth. The flowers attract birds and bees, and the shrubby growth gives shelter for small birds. Adaptable to a range of situations and climates, it can tolerate moderate frosts once established. **Climate:** Cool to warm temperate, Mediterranean, subtropical. **Soil:** Moist to well-drained; clayey, loamy or sandy.

1–10 m
1–5 m

52. *Callistemon salignus* (willow bottlebrush) D+W

A very versatile plant, the willow bottlebrush is a lovely ornamental that can tolerate both wet and dry conditions, making it useful for difficult spots. The soft red new growth and cream to pale yellow flowers make it an attractive plant throughout the year. Growing to a large shrub or small tree, it can develop an invasive root system so it should be planted well away from buildings. The willow-like foliage and papery bark are lovely features of this plant. It is great for attracting wildlife, too. **Climate:** Arid, cool to warm temperate, Mediterranean, semi-arid, subtropical. **Soil:** Poor to well-drained; clayey, loamy or sandy.

0.3–0.6 m
0.2–0.3 m

53. *Calostemma purpureum* (garland lily)

A beautiful native lily with bright pink flowers, this is found naturally on the east coast and in southern Australia but is now rare in its native habitats. It is a wonderful garden plant, adaptable and low maintenance, with a rewarding flower display in summer. A clumping perennial, it has strappy leaves and looks great planted in containers and rockeries. **Climate:** Cool to warm temperate, Mediterranean, semi-arid, subtropical. **Soil:** Moist to well-drained; clayey, loamy or sandy.

1.5–2.5 m
1.5–2.5 m

54. *Calothamnus quadrifidus* (one-sided bottlebrush) D

The one-sided bottlebrush is similar to *Callistemon* species, with bird-attracting flowers on a tough and drought-tolerant shrub. The fringed crimson flowers contrast beautifully against the dense dark green foliage. It makes a great screen or windbreak, as well as a good hedging plant. Adaptable to a range of soils, it does appreciate good drainage and this will improve growth, but it can also tolerate moist soils. Prune it often and feed with native fertiliser to keep it dense and bushy. **Climate:** Cool to warm temperate, Mediterranean. **Soil:** Poor to well-drained; clayey, loamy or sandy.

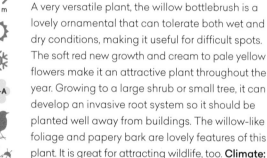

55. *Calytrix tetragona* (fringe myrtle)

1–2.5 m
0.5–1.5 m

The fringe myrtle features abundant white or pink star-shaped flowers on long stems, and they are great as cut flowers. The small leaves have a pleasant spicy scent when crushed. It is easy to grow and a tough plant for the garden, suited to positions in light shade to full sun. It likes a well-drained soil and can be grown in raised beds for better drainage. Tip pruning will encourage denser growth and more flowers. Feed it with a native fertiliser in spring to keep it healthy. **Climate:** Cool to warm temperate, Mediterranean, semi-arid. **Soil:** Well-drained; loamy or sandy.

56. *Carpobrotus rossii* (karkalla, pigface)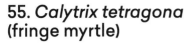

0.2–0.4 m
1–3 m

A wonderful drought-tolerant plant with many uses, karkalla is native to coastal areas and has succulent leaves and bright flowers. Often seen growing on sand dunes, it is a great ground cover for stabilising sandy soils. Tolerant of salt and dry conditions, it is fast growing and can grow to a few metres wide. The fleshy fruits are edible when fully ripe, and the leaves are also edible. Perfect for coastal gardens and exposed positions, it should be grown in well-drained soil in part-shade to full sun. **Climate:** Cool to warm temperate, Mediterranean, semi-arid, subtropical. **Soil:** Well-drained; clayey, loamy or sandy, saline soil.

57. *Chamelaucium uncinatum* (Geraldton wax)

2–5 m
2–6 m

Geraldton wax is a beautiful native flower, often used in floral arrangements for its waxy pink flowers as they last well when cut and provide a pretty pastel colour. The fine foliage is aromatic when crushed, adding a lovely scent to bouquets. It is a tough plant in the garden, forming a dense shrub that works well as a screen or feature plant for its stunning display of flowers. Native to dry climates, it does best in areas with hot dry summers and needs a well-drained soil. It is tolerant of drought once established. Prune lightly after flowering. **Climate:** Cool to warm temperate, Mediterranean, semi-arid. **Soil:** Well-drained; loamy or sandy.

58. *Chrysocephalum apiculatum* (yellow buttons)

0.2–0.3 m
0.4–0.5 m

A ground cover with golden yellow button flowers set against soft silvery green foliage, this is a lovely and tough native. It looks particularly good when planted en masse, and also works well as a border, in rockeries or in containers. Flowering throughout the year, it will brighten up any space. Full sun and a well-drained soil are the best conditions for this plant. **Climate:** Cool to warm temperate, Mediterranean. **Soil:** Well-drained; clayey, loamy or sandy, saline soil.

59. *Cissus antarctica* (kangaroo vine)

0.3–4 m
0.5–6 m

A dense climber that also makes a great indoor plant, kangaroo vine has lovely deep green foliage with a copper colour on new growth. The curling tendrils stretch out to help it climb, so give it some support or grow it as a ground cover. Happy in a range of conditions, it grows well in light to full shade. Native to the east coast, it is a vigorous plant but can be pruned as much as necessary. **Climate:** Warm temperate, Mediterranean, subtropical. **Soil:** Moist to well-drained; loamy or sandy.

60. *Conospermum caeruleum* (blue smoke bush)

0.4–1 m
0.5–1 m

This is a low shrub with beautiful blue flowers that are sometimes grown for cut-flower production. The flowers appear in profusion during winter and spring. An adaptable plant, it naturally grows in areas that regularly flood, so it is tolerant of both dry and boggy soils. It is not seen often in cultivation, but it is a lovely drought-tolerant ornamental. **Climate:** Warm temperate, Mediterranean. **Soil:** Poor to well-drained; clayey, loamy or sandy.

61. *Conostylis aculeata* (prickly conostylis)

0.1–0.6 m

0.3–1 m

A great plant for dry gardens, this grassy perennial has bright yellow flowers. It is a very low-maintenance plant that blooms for a long period, perfect for flower gardens and container growing. A well-drained sandy soil is ideal, though it is adaptable to a range of soils. It grows from rhizomes that will slowly multiply in the garden, or they can be divided into new plants. **Climate:** Cool to warm temperate, Mediterranean, semi-arid. **Soil:** Well-drained; clayey, loamy or sandy.

62. *Coronidium elatum* 'Sunny Side Up'

1–1.5 m

1–1.5 m

This everlasting daisy cultivar has abundant white flowers that stay on the plant for months, and they can be used as cut flowers, too. With soft deep green foliage and a shrubby habit, it is a beautiful feature plant in the garden and looks lovely grown in containers. Deadhead flowers in late spring to give the plant more vigour and to improve flowering the following season. **Climate:** Cool to warm temperate, semi-arid, subtropical. **Soil:** Well-drained; clayey, loamy or sandy.

63. *Correa alba* (white correa)

1–1.5 m

1–1.5 m

A tough shrub native to coastal areas of eastern Australia, the white correa is a low-maintenance ornamental that provides nectar and shelter for wildlife. The foliage is a soft greyish green, and the small white flowers appear in autumn and winter. Perfect for coastal gardens as it tolerates salty winds, it flowers best in full sun but will grow in light shade. It responds well to pruning and can be shaped into different forms. **Climate:** Cool to warm temperate, Mediterranean. **Soil:** Well-drained; clayey, loamy or sandy.

64. *Correa pulchella*

0.8–1 m

0.5–1 m

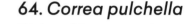

This beautiful correa varies from prostrate to 1 metre in height, and has bell-shaped flowers in orange or red tones. The flowers appear in autumn and winter, and they attract nectar-eating birds to the garden. Adaptable to most soil types, it is best in full sun to light shade. Tip pruning the plant when young will increase flowering, and it should be trimmed after flowering. It needs a well-drained soil, and some native fertiliser in spring will help it thrive. **Climate:** Cool to warm temperate, Mediterranean. **Soil:** Well-drained; clayey, loamy or sandy.

65. *Correa reflexa* (native fuchsia)

0.5–1.2 m

0.5–1 m

A hardy low-growing shrub, the native fuchsia flowers all year. This makes it a great wildlife-garden plant, as it provides nectar throughout the various seasons. It is variable in habit and flower colour, and a number of different forms have been recognised. The flowers can be greenish yellow, pink, or red and green. It grows in a range of soils and tolerates part-shade or full sun, but will do best with morning sun and a sandy well-drained soil. Tip prune after the main spring flowering period to promote dense and healthy growth. **Climate:** Cool, cool to warm temperate, Mediterranean. **Soil:** Well-drained; clayey, loamy or sandy.

66. *Corymbia ficifolia* 'Wildfire'

4–6 m

3–4 m

1–2

A spectacular small tree, this flowering gum cultivar has lovely dark green leaves and red-tinged new growth in spring and summer. It puts on a vibrant display when in flower, lighting up the plant with large scarlet flowers that attract nectar-eating birds. It can be grown in most climates, and plants sold now are grafted to better tolerate humidity. Position the plant in full sun in a well-drained soil for best results. **Climate:** Cool, cool to warm temperate, Mediterranean. **Soil:** Well-drained; clayey, loamy or sandy.

67. *Cupaniopsis anacardioides* (tuckeroo)

This is an attractive small tree with dark green leaves and interesting orange seed pods that are loved by native birds. Excellent for coastal areas in warm climates, the tuckeroo has a spreading crown and makes a good shade tree. It is a lovely ornamental, often planted as a street tree. Low maintenance and generally free of pests and diseases, it is a great waterwise tree for larger gardens. **Climate:** Cool to warm temperate, Mediterranean, subtropical. **Soil:** Moist to well-drained; clayey, loamy or sandy, saline soil.

68. *Cymbopogon ambiguus* (native lemongrass)

A relative of the culinary lemongrass, native lemongrass is a tough grassy plant that is very easy to grow. It has pleasant scented leaves that are used to make tea and for steam inhalation; First Nations peoples used them to treat chest infections and sores. Recent research has shown that the tea is useful for headaches and migraines as well. The grassy clumps grow to a couple of metres high with delicate seed heads, and trimming the foliage stimulates the plant to produce new flushes of growth. **Climate:** Warm temperate, Mediterranean, semi-arid, subtropical. **Soil:** Moist to well-drained; clayey, loamy or sandy.

69. *Cymbopogon refractus* (barbed wire grass)

An attractive native grass in the lemongrass family, barbed wire grass gets its common name from the shape of its decorative seed heads. The crushed foliage has a lemon scent. It is excellent for poor soils and dry regions, and very useful for revegetating eroded areas. It is also great for landscaping, as it is drought-tolerant and is ornamental when the seed heads are on display. **Climate:** Cool to warm temperate, Mediterranean, semi-arid, subtropical. **Soil:** Well-drained; clayey, loamy or sandy, poor soil.

70. *Darwinia citriodora* (lemon-scented myrtle)

This dense shrub has aromatic dark green foliage and deep red flowers that contrast beautifully against the leaves. Native to southern Western Australia, this plant likes a sandy, well-drained soil in a position with dappled light, though it will withstand full sun, too. The lemon-scented leaves release a lovely fragrance when crushed. Flowers appear in winter and spring (and into summer in some areas), and they attract honeyeaters and native bees to the garden. **Climate:** Cool to warm temperate, Mediterranean. **Soil:** Moist to well-drained; loamy or sandy.

71. *Dendrobium speciosum*, syn. *Thelychiton speciosus* (rock orchid)

The rock orchid grows as an epiphyte or lithophyte, meaning that it naturally grows on other plants or on rocks. It cannot be grown in soil, and should be grown on a tree branch or positioned between rocks and secured in place with twine or wire. The roots will take up nutrients from the decaying leaf litter around them. It can also be planted in a container in a coarse orchid potting mix. Position it in good sunlight for best flowering, and feed with a liquid fertiliser during the warmer months. **Climate:** Warm temperate, Mediterranean, subtropical. **Soil:** Very well-drained; orchid potting mix.

72. *Dianella caerulea* (blue flax lily)

This is a tough strappy perennial, with delicate blue flowers and vibrant, edible, bluish violet berries. The flowers grow on tall stems above the foliage in spring and summer. Native to eastern Australia, it is great for coastal gardens and for stabilising sandy soils. Very low maintenance and drought-tolerant once established, it is a versatile ornamental suited to a range of uses. It can be pruned back when needed, regrowing from underground rhizomes. **Climate:** Cool to warm temperate, Mediterranean, subtropical. **Soil:** Moist to well-drained; clayey, loamy or sandy, saline soil.

73. *Diplopeltis huegelii* (pepper flower)

0.5–1.5 m
0.5–1.5 m

A lovely low shrub with pale delicate flowers, the pepper flower is wonderful when planted en masse in native flower gardens, or grown in containers. Native to Western Australia, it is tolerant of drought and grows well in a range of soils, from rocky to clayey and sandy soils. The flowers appear from winter through to the middle of summer, attracting bees and insects to the garden. It is a great ornamental for warm dry climates and water-efficient native gardens. **Climate:** Cool to warm temperate, Mediterranean, semi-arid. **Soil:** Moist to well-drained; clayey, loamy or sandy, poor soil.

74. *Disphyma crassifolium* (roundleaf pigface)

0.2–0.3 m
0.5–1 m

A very useful native succulent, this plant is both edible and highly tolerant of drought. The fleshy leaves have a salty flavour and can be used fresh, in stir-fries and for pickling. It is great for stabilising soil in coastal areas, as it tolerates salinity very well. The succulent leaves are a fire retardant, so it can be planted around houses in areas prone to bushfire. It is suitable for growing in hanging baskets and containers where the leaves can be harvested often. Vibrant pink flowers appear all year. **Climate:** Arid, cool to warm temperate, Mediterranean, semi-arid. **Soil:** Well-drained; clayey, loamy or sandy, poor soil, saline soil.

75. *Doryanthes excelsa* (Gymea lily)

2–4 m
2–3 m

The Gymea lily is a striking ornamental plant native to the Central Coast and Sydney area of New South Wales. It is an impressive plant with very large sword-shaped leaves and a prominent flower stem (2–4 metres tall!) with deep red flowers on top. It has a clumping habit and a beautiful architectural form. This plant needs deep soil to thrive, as it buries its underground stem deep in the ground to survive drought and fire, but it can also be grown in large containers. **Climate:** Cool to warm temperate, Mediterranean, subtropical. **Soil:** Moist to well-drained; clayey, loamy or sandy, poor soil.

76. *Doryanthes palmeri* (spear lily)

1–3 m
1.5–3 m

Closely related to the Gymea lily but featuring an arched flower stem, the spear lily is native to northern New South Wales and Queensland. The flowers form along the end of the stem, causing it to droop from the weight. Useful for architectural and landscape design, it is a tall and sculptural plant with long pointed leaves. It can also be grown in large containers. Prune off old flower heads once they are finished, and trim any dying leaves from the plant in autumn to keep it in shape. **Climate:** Cool to warm temperate, Mediterranean, subtropical. **Soil:** Moist to well-drained; clayey, loamy or sandy, poor soil.

77. *Elaeocarpus reticulatus* 'Prima Donna'

8–10 m
3–4 m

This smaller cultivar of the blueberry ash is a wonderfully versatile shrub or tree, native to warmer areas of Australia's east coast. A handsome plant with pale pink flowers and dark green leaves, the flowers and small blue fruits are often on the plant at the same time, providing a lovely colour contrast. The flowers are fringed with fine petals and are sometimes described as 'fairy petticoats'. They have an anise-like fragrance. The regent bowerbird collects the fruits because of their blue colour, and the fruits are eaten by other birds. **Climate:** Warm temperate, Mediterranean, subtropical. **Soil:** Moist to well-drained; clayey, loamy or sandy, poor soil.

78. *Enchylaena tomentosa* (ruby saltbush)

0.4–1 m
0.5–1 m

A fantastic drought-tolerant shrub, this small plant bears edible berries that eventually turn from green to red, standing out against the lovely grey-green foliage. This foliage is covered in tiny white hairs that help the plant survive drought conditions. It is very versatile, growing in inland areas with sandy and saline soils, as well as withstanding frost. It can also grow in sand-dune environments, withstanding salty and sand-laden winds. **Climate:** Arid, cool, cool to warm temperate, Mediterranean, semi-arid, subtropical, tropical. **Soil:** Moist to well-drained, dry; clayey, loamy or sandy, poor soil, saline soil.

↑ 0.1–0.2 m
↔ 1–2 m

AY

79. *Eremophila glabra* 'Kalbarri Carpet'  Ⓓ

This beautiful ground cover has golden yellow flowers that contrast well with the soft silvery foliage. It flowers mainly in the warmer months, and spot flowers in the cooler months. The flowers attract nectar-eating creatures, and the plant's dense form provides habitat, too. Ideal for areas with low humidity, it is a low-maintenance plant that is tolerant of frost and drought. It grows well in containers and looks great planted on banks and walls, or plant in groups for landscaping larger areas. **Climate:** Cool to warm temperate, Mediterranean, semi-arid. **Soil:** Well-drained, dry; clayey, loamy or sandy, poor soil.

↑ 0.8–2 m
↔ 0.5–2 m

W–S

80. *Eremophila nivea* (silky emu bush)

A small to medium shrub with striking silver foliage, this *Eremophila* needs dry conditions to thrive in the long term. It has purple flowers from late winter to early summer, and it makes a wonderful feature shrub because of its lovely foliage that stands out in the garden. This plant is from dry climates in Western Australia, so it is usually grafted for growing on the east coast. Plant it in a pot or raised bed to provide the best drainage, and keep the foliage as dry as possible to help prevent diseases. **Climate:** Cool to warm temperate, Mediterranean, semi-arid. **Soil:** Well-drained, dry; clayey, loamy or sandy, poor soil.

↑ 0.4–0.7 m
↔ 0.4–0.8 m

S

81. *Eryngium ovinum* (blue devil)

The spiky, blue, thistle-like flowers of this plant make it a great addition to the garden, and they also work wonderfully as cut flowers, either fresh or dried. The flowers last for several weeks on the plant. It is a perennial that grows from late winter, flowers in summer and then dies down in autumn. It has a large taproot and will resprout again in late winter. It is native to woodlands and grasslands throughout southern regions of Australia. Preferring a well-drained soil, the blue devil needs a full-sun position in order to thrive. **Climate:** Cool to warm temperate, Mediterranean, semi-arid. **Soil:** Well-drained, dry; clayey, loamy or sandy, poor soil.

↑ 6–9 m
↔ 3–4 m
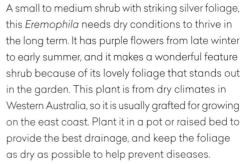
WSp

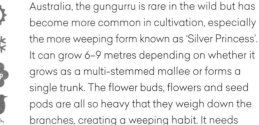

82. *Eucalyptus caesia* (gungurru)

A spectacular and graceful tree from Western Australia, the gungurru is rare in the wild but has become more common in cultivation, especially the more weeping form known as 'Silver Princess'. It can grow 6–9 metres depending on whether it grows as a multi-stemmed mallee or forms a single trunk. The flower buds, flowers and seed pods are all so heavy that they weigh down the branches, creating a weeping habit. It needs protection from winds and a spot in plenty of sun with a well-drained soil. **Climate:** Cool to warm temperate, Mediterranean, semi-arid. **Soil:** Well-drained; clayey, loamy or sandy, poor soil.

↑ 3–8 m
↔ 2–6 m
SA

83. *Eucalyptus erythrocorys* (illyarrie)

A small mallee from Western Australia, this has eye-catching crimson flower buds that open to bright yellow flowers from late summer to autumn. The flowers are followed by large and interesting gumnuts that give the tree added ornamental effect throughout the year. It can grow to an untidy form but responds well to pruning, so it can be shaped to suit a range of spaces. The gumnuts can weigh down the branches, giving the tree a weeping appearance. It is one of the most striking eucalypts when in flower, and it attracts many birds. **Climate:** Warm temperate, Mediterranean, semi-arid. **Soil:** Well-drained; loamy or sandy.

↑ 10–30 m
↔ 4–8 m
S

84. *Eucalyptus gunnii* (cider gum)

The cider gum is a medium to large tree native to Tasmania, and it is one of the fastest-growing eucalypts. As it is known for its high cold tolerance, it is grown in parts of Western Europe and Great Britain. The juvenile foliage can be used for flower arranging, with the silvery blue leaves lasting well in the vase. The plant has a fresh eucalyptus smell from the oils in the leaves. It grows to quite a large tree if left unchecked, but it can be pruned to keep it shrubby and so it continually produces the ornamental young foliage. **Climate:** Cool, cool to warm temperate, Mediterranean, semi-arid. **Soil:** Well-drained; clayey, loamy or sandy.

85. *Eutaxia obovata* (egg and bacon plant)

This is a small dense shrub that puts on an abundant display of golden yellow-and-maroon pea flowers in spring. The flowers last well on the plant, have a very slight fragrance, and attract bees and butterflies to the garden. It can be planted as a colourful hedge or screen plant, as well as in containers. Grow in light shade to full sun, choosing a site that gives it shelter from the drying afternoon sun. It is tolerant of drought and frost once established. **Climate:** Cool to warm temperate, Mediterranean, semi-arid. **Soil:** Well-drained; clayey, loamy or sandy.

86. *Goodenia ovata* 'Gold Cover'

This new *Goodenia* cultivar is a versatile fast-growing ground cover with deep green leaves plus bright yellow flowers in the warmer seasons. Plant it en masse as a ground cover, grow it in containers to spill out over edges, or plant it at the top of walls and banks to trail down. It is a tough plant that tolerates drought well and can withstand light frosts. Prune lightly to maintain shape and encourage more dense growth. **Climate:** Cool to warm temperate, Mediterranean, subtropical. **Soil:** Moist to well-drained, dry; clayey, loamy or sandy.

87. *Gossypium sturtianum* (Sturt's desert rose)

A highly drought-tolerant plant, Sturt's desert rose is a woody shrub from dry inland regions of Australia featuring large lilac flowers similar to hibiscus. It is the floral emblem of the Northern Territory. The large flowers are highly attractive to honeyeaters. Adapted to hot dry conditions, it is somewhat versatile and can grow in humid areas but needs excellent drainage so the roots do not become waterlogged. Position in full sun in a spot with good air circulation to discourage fungal problems. **Climate:** Arid, cool to warm temperate, Mediterranean, semi-arid, subtropical. **Soil:** Well-drained, dry; clayey, loamy or sandy, poor soil.

88. *Grevillea* 'Blood Orange'

With similar characteristics to other large-flowering grevilleas, this plant has the outstanding feature of distinctive deep orange flowers that appear year-round. The flowers make this a highly attractive plant to birds. It can be pruned after flowering to create a denser form, or it can be left unpruned to grow into more of a large shrub or small tree. It is adaptable to a range of circumstances, especially drought and coastal conditions, while still providing excellent screening. **Climate:** Cool, cool to warm temperate, Mediterranean. **Soil:** Well-drained; clayey, loamy or sandy.

89. *Grevillea* 'Bronze Rover'

This grevillea is a wonderful ground cover, with a dense habit and attractive bronze-coloured new growth. The flowers are bright red and can be used as cut flowers; they also attract nectar-eating birds and wildlife. A great choice for landscaping or to cover low embankments, it is a low-maintenance plant that can withstand drought once it is established. It is also frost hardy and fast growing. Plant it in a well-drained soil in a sunny or part-shade position. **Climate:** Cool, cool to warm temperate, Mediterranean. **Soil:** Well-drained; clayey, loamy or sandy.

90. *Grevillea crithmifolia*

This is a low shrub with a dense growth habit plus abundant white flowers in winter and spring. The delicate flowers are scented and attract nectar-eating wildlife to the garden. It makes a great ground cover to keep weeds down, or it can be grown as a feature plant in a native garden. It does not need much maintenance apart from a light pruning after flowering to maintain bushy growth. Once established, it tolerates drought and frost well. **Climate:** Cool, cool to warm temperate, Mediterranean, semi-arid. **Soil:** Well-drained; clayey, loamy or sandy.

91. *Grevillea eriostachya* (yellow flame grevillea)

1.5–2 m
1–2 m

A medium to large shrub, this is a striking plant when in flower with large green flower buds opening to bright golden yellow flowers. The flower stems stand tall above the foliage. This grevillea is one for drier climates, as it is native to desert regions of Australia; it is difficult to maintain in humid climates unless it is grafted. In dry areas, the plant flowers in response to rainfall, but in other areas it flowers for many months with a peak in spring. The flowers contain so much nectar that it sometimes drips onto the ground. **Climate:** Arid, cool to warm temperate, Mediterranean, semi-arid. **Soil:** Well-drained, dry; loamy or sandy.

92. *Grevillea* 'Goldfever'

0.3–0.4 m
1–1.5 m

'Goldfever' is a low dense shrub with a spreading growth habit, making it excellent as a ground cover, in pots or in rockeries. It produces light golden yellow spider-like flowers throughout the year, providing nectar for all kinds of wildlife. It is a very low-maintenance plant and tolerant of a range of soil types, including heavy soils. It withstands drought and frost once established. It is an excellent plant for native, low-maintenance and water-smart gardens. **Climate:** Cool, cool to warm temperate, Mediterranean, semi-arid. **Soil:** Well-drained; clayey, loamy or sandy.

93. *Grevillea lanigera* (woolly grevillea)

0.5–1.5 m
0.4–1.5 m

This is a low-maintenance shrub that can be variable in form, with one of the most common forms available being a prostrate spreading shrub. It has clustered flowers in shades of red or pink that appear throughout the year but most heavily in winter and spring. The small hairy leaves give it some drought tolerance when young, and it is quite tolerant of drought once established. If given a well-drained soil, it is an adaptable plant that can thrive in a range of situations. Prune lightly when required to keep it in shape. **Climate:** Cool, cool to warm temperate, Mediterranean. **Soil:** Well-drained, dry; clayey, loamy or sandy.

94. *Grevillea leucopteris* (old socks)

2–3 m
1–2 m

A grevillea from Western Australia, this one is highly ornamental because it bears flowers on tall canes that stand well above the foliage. The flower spikes and flowers are striking, though the flowers smell quite unpleasant (hence the common name). The scent is attractive to pollinators, however, so this is a good plant for wildlife. A tall shrub, it has soft fern-like foliage and pink-coloured new growth. It dislikes humidity but can be grown as a graft in more humid climates like those found on the east coast of Australia. **Climate:** Arid, cool to warm temperate, Mediterranean, semi-arid. **Soil:** Well-drained, dry; loamy or sandy.

95. *Grevillea* 'Moonlight'

3–5 m
2–4 m

A very easy-to-grow and rewarding grevillea, this cultivar produces flowers all year round, as well as being a hardy and adaptable plant. Growing into a large shrub or small tree, it makes a good screening and hedging plant. It can also be grown as a feature plant for its outstanding flower display. Prune after flowering to encourage dense growth, or cut the flowers to display in vases. **Climate:** Cool, cool to warm temperate, Mediterranean, semi-arid, subtropical. **Soil:** Well-drained, dry; clayey, loamy or sandy, poor soil.

96. *Hakea decurrens* 'Pink Lace'

1.8–2.2 m
1.5–2 m

This hakea has gorgeous scented flowers in shades of soft pink, appearing in winter and spring. There is also a white-flowered form of *Hakea decurrens*. The pink form is a medium shrub with prickly foliage, and it provides shelter and nectar to small native birds. The branches also have a lovely weeping habit. It can be used as a screening or hedging plant and is great for habitat gardens. **Climate:** Cool to warm temperate, Mediterranean. **Soil:** Well-drained; clayey, loamy or sandy.

97. *Hakea laurina* (pincushion hakea)

2.5–6 m

2–5 m

This is a large shrub or small tree with spectacular red-and-cream pincushion flowers and attractive foliage. Originally from south-western Western Australia, it is an adaptable plant in cultivation and has become naturalised in parts of south-eastern Australia – so make sure it is not an environmental weed in your area. Grow it in full sun for best flowering, and ensure that the soil is well-drained. It may need staking in windy conditions, as it has a shallow root system. **Climate:** Cool to warm temperate, Mediterranean. **Soil:** Well-drained; clayey, loamy or sandy, poor soil.

98. *Hakea victoria* (royal hakea)

2–3 m

1–1.5 m

A striking plant with tough multicoloured foliage, this Western Australian hakea makes a wonderful feature plant. The serrated leaves are thick and leathery, with shades of deep orange, red and green, growing on tall stems that can reach 3 metres. The diminutive cream flowers appear in spring, nestled among the leaves. It performs best in areas with low humidity and needs full sun and a well-drained soil. **Climate:** Cool to warm temperate, Mediterranean. **Soil:** Well-drained, dry; clayey, loamy or sandy.

99. *Hardenbergia violacea* (native sarsaparilla)

1–3 m

1–2 m

This is a tough and vigorous climber or ground cover with clusters of small violet pea flowers from the middle of winter and into spring. There are a number of different forms of this plant available, including pink- and white-flowered forms. Grow the plant on a frame or trellis to encourage it to climb, or plant it as a ground cover or cascading down walls. It can be pruned hard to keep it growing as a shrub, or left to wander. **Climate:** Cool to warm temperate, Mediterranean, subtropical. **Soil:** Well-drained; clayey, loamy or sandy, poor soil.

100. *Hibbertia scandens* (climbing guinea flower)

0.5–3 m

1–5 m

This plant is a vigorous climber with bright yellow flowers, and it makes a great ground cover or screen to cover fences, walls or embankments. It is excellent for coastal gardens, as it can tolerate salt and sandy soils. An easy-to-care-for plant, all it needs is a trim to remove any rogue branches. It is tolerant of drought once established and adaptable to a range of conditions. Grow it in full sun to promote more flowering. **Climate:** Cool to warm temperate, Mediterranean, subtropical. **Soil:** Moist to well-drained, dry; clayey, loamy or sandy, poor soil.

101. *Hypocalymma angustifolium* (pink-flowered myrtle)

1–1.5 m

1–1.5 m

This small shrub has ornamental flowers in spring that can be used in flower arranging, lasting well in a vase or when dried. The delicate flowers occur in shades of cream and pink darkening to red, and they are clustered along the stems. The slender leaves have a sweetly spicy scent when crushed. It is drought-tolerant once established, but will do better with regular watering. It needs a sheltered position protected from strong winds, and requires annual pruning after flowering to promote dense growth. **Climate:** Cool to warm temperate, Mediterranean. **Soil:** Well-drained; loamy or sandy.

102. *Hypocalymma robustum* (Swan River myrtle)

1–1.5 m

1–1.5 m

A great shrub for Mediterranean climates, this elegant plant bears clusters of pink flowers along the stems in winter and spring, putting on an outstanding display. It makes a great compact feature plant for regions with dry summers, but it doesn't cope as well with humid climates and summer rainfall. Plant it in a well-drained soil in full sun or dappled shade, and prune after flowering to promote dense growth. **Climate:** Warm temperate, Mediterranean. **Soil:** Well-drained; loamy or sandy.

103

104

105

106

107

108

103. *Isopogon anemonifolius* 'Little Drumsticks'

0.3–0.7 m
0.5–0.8 m

A great compact ornamental for small gardens or mass plantings, this low dense shrub has attractive foliage and bright yellow drumstick flowers throughout winter and spring. It is a good plant for growing in courtyard containers or planting in groups for a larger flower display. The sunny yellow flowers attract a range of small native birds to the garden. They can also be used as cut flowers. It needs a moist well-drained soil in light shade to full sun. **Climate:** Cool to warm temperate, Mediterranean, subtropical. **Soil:** Moist to well-drained; loamy or sandy.

104. *Kennedia nigricans* (black coral pea)

0.2–10 m
1–10 m
W–S
1–2

With its unusual black-and-yellow flowers and large deep green leaves, this vigorous climber or ground cover is a spectacular addition to any garden. It makes a great feature plant, and it can be used as a screen to cover fences and bare patches in the garden. It is adaptable to a range of soils and prefers a sheltered position in light shade to full sun. Ensure that the root system has a thick layer of mulch to keep moisture in, and prune after flowering to encourage dense growth. **Climate:** Cool to warm temperate, Mediterranean. **Soil:** Well-drained; loamy or sandy.

105. *Kunzea ambigua* (white kunzea)

1–5 m
1–3 m

White kunzea is a lovely aromatic shrub with masses of small cream flowers in spring that attract nectar-loving insects and birds. It is a small- to medium-sized shrub, good for screening and low-maintenance gardens. Naturally occurring along the east coast of Australia, it is a tough plant that can adapt to a range of conditions and is tolerant of drought and poor soils. An easy-care plant, it can be pruned after flowering to maintain a dense and bushy growth habit. **Climate:** Cool, cool to warm temperate, Mediterranean. **Soil:** Moist to well-drained, dry; clayey, loamy or sandy, poor soil.

106. *Kunzea pomifera* (muntries)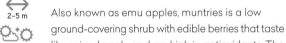

0.3–0.5 m
2–5 m

Also known as emu apples, muntries is a low ground-covering shrub with edible berries that taste like spiced apple and are high in antioxidants. The crunchy berries turn from green to a deep maroon when ripe. It is a low-maintenance plant, and it can be trellised to make harvesting the fruits easier. It doesn't like root disturbance, so make sure to mulch well when planting. Consistent watering while the plant is flowering and fruiting will help it to become established and to perform well. **Climate:** Cool, cool to warm temperate, Mediterranean. **Soil:** Moist to well-drained, dry; clayey, loamy or sandy, poor soil.

107. *Lasiopetalum baueri* 'Prostrate'

0.5–0.6 m
1–2 m

An attractive ground cover, this plant has rust-coloured new growth plus lovely pink flowers in winter and spring. This particular form has a dense prostrate habit and is great for keeping weeds down. The flowers are excellent for dried-flower arrangements. Grow in a well-drained soil in full sun for best results. A tough plant, it is perfect for drought-tolerant and coastal gardens. **Climate:** Cool to warm temperate, Mediterranean. **Soil:** Well-drained, dry; clayey, loamy or sandy, saline soil.

108. *Lepidozamia peroffskyana* (pineapple zamia)

3–7 m
2–4 m

A low-maintenance and impressive cycad with palm-like fronds, the pineapple zamia makes a great feature plant and can even be grown indoors in a bright position. A slow-growing and long-lived plant that is tolerant of drought, it is a great landscaping plant and also does well in containers. Grow it in a sunny or dappled shade position but protect it from the hot afternoon sun, as this can burn the leaves. It doesn't need fertiliser and is mostly free of pests. **Climate:** Cool to warm temperate, Mediterranean. **Soil:** Moist to well-drained, dry; clayey, loamy or sandy.

109. *Leptospermum flavescens* 'Cardwell'

With a weeping habit, abundant flowering and aromatic foliage, this tea-tree cultivar makes a beautiful feature plant or informal screen. It is a large fast-growing shrub that can be pruned to keep it smaller. From late winter through spring, the weeping branches are completely covered in small white flowers, turning the plant almost white. It can be grown in light shade, but full sun will encourage the best flowering. It prefers a well-drained soil and is tolerant of drought once established. **Climate:** Cool, cool to warm temperate, Mediterranean, subtropical. **Soil:** Well-drained; clayey, loamy or sandy, saline soil.

110. *Leptospermum* 'Pink Cascade'

This tea-tree cultivar has a low habit and lovely weeping form, with masses of soft pink flowers covering the plant in spring. Growing to under a metre high, it is perfect for embankments and rockeries where the beautiful arched branches will cascade down over the side. It can be grown in part-shade to full sun, and prefers a moist well-drained soil. It can withstand light frost and is tolerant of drought once established. It is an adaptable and highly ornamental cultivar suited to a range of soil conditions. **Climate:** Cool to warm temperate, Mediterranean, subtropical. **Soil:** Moist to well-drained; clayey, loamy or sandy, poor soil.

111. *Leptospermum rotundifolium* 'Julie Ann'

With dense foliage and a spreading habit, this tea-tree cultivar is great for creating thickets to keep weeds down and to provide habitat in the garden. It is a prostrate form that makes a great ground cover or spreading shrub to cover banks or spill over walls. The flowers appear in autumn and winter, starting out a deep purple-pink before softening to a lighter shade of pink. It prefers a well-drained soil in full sun but can tolerate heavier clay soils and part-shade as well. It doesn't require pruning to keep a dense form. **Climate:** Cool to warm temperate, Mediterranean, subtropical. **Soil:** Moist to well-drained; clayey, loamy or sandy.

112. *Leucophyta brownii* (cushion bush)

This is a tough and useful shrub with ornamental grey-green foliage plus golden ball-shaped flowers appearing in summer. With its soft textured foliage and naturally rounded growth habit, it is perfect for low-maintenance gardens and for filling difficult parts of the garden. An excellent plant for coastal sites, it is very tolerant of salt and windy conditions. It is also tolerant of drought and adaptable to most soil types. **Climate:** Cool, cool to warm temperate, Mediterranean, semi-arid. **Soil:** Moist to well-drained, dry; clayey, loamy or sandy, poor soil, saline soil.

113. *Lomandra* 'Lime Tuff'

The perfect low-maintenance shrub for drought-tolerant gardens, this hybrid has bright green foliage and cream flower spikes in spring. It is adaptable to a range of climates and requires almost no maintenance to keep it looking good. It can be cut back to the ground and will resprout from its underground rhizome. It can tolerate heavy frosts, coastal conditions and drought. Use it as a border plant, under trees or as a general landscaping plant. **Climate:** Cool, cool to warm temperate, Mediterranean, semi-arid, subtropical. **Soil:** Moist to well-drained, dry; clayey, loamy or sandy, poor soil.

114. *Melaleuca bracteata* 'Revolution Gold'

The outstanding feature of this cultivar is its deep golden foliage, which can create contrast in the garden. It is a large shrub or small tree that can be used as a feature plant for its bright foliage, or planted alongside shrubs with darker foliage to offset the golden leaves. Moderately tolerant of drought once established, it prefers a well-drained soil and full sun to encourage a more intense colour in the foliage. It bears small white flowers in spring and summer, and it should be pruned after flowering to encourage a dense form. **Climate:** Cool to warm temperate, Mediterranean. **Soil:** Well-drained; clayey, loamy or sandy, poor soil.

115. *Melaleuca conothamnoides*

1–2 m
1–2 m

A striking Western Australian plant, this is a compact low shrub with bold pink miniature bottlebrush flowers in spring. The flowers contrast beautifully with the grey-green foliage. It is highly ornamental and makes a great feature plant that also brings nectar-eating birds to the garden. Grow it in full sun in a light well-drained soil, and prune lightly after flowering. **Climate:** Cool to warm temperate, Mediterranean. **Soil:** Well-drained; loamy or sandy, poor soil.

116. *Melaleuca decussata* 'Dwarf'

1.2–1.5 m
0.5–0.8 m

This dwarf shrub features small bottlebrush flowers in mauve as well as tiny grey-green leaves covering the stems. The flowers appear in spring. It self-seeds readily so is useful for hedging, but it can be an environmental weed in some parts of Victoria. Grow it in full sun to stop it becoming sparse and woody. Plant it in a well-drained soil, and trim after flowering. **Climate:** Cool to warm temperate, Mediterranean. **Soil:** Well-drained; clayey, loamy or sandy.

117. *Melaleuca diosmifolia* (green honey myrtle)

2–3 m
2–3 m

With unusual lime green bottlebrush flowers, the green honey myrtle is a lovely ornamental shrub from Western Australia. It has a naturally compact growth habit and small leaves covering the stems. Growing to a few metres in height and width, it is a good screening shrub or windbreak and is suitable for coastal areas. A well-drained soil is essential, and it tolerates light frost. The flowers attract nectar-eating birds to the garden. **Climate:** Warm temperate, Mediterranean. **Soil:** Well-drained; loamy or sandy, saline soil.

118. *Melaleuca fulgens* (scarlet honey myrtle)

1–3 m
1.5–3 m

The striking scarlet bottlebrush flowers are the highlight of this Western Australian shrub. It is attractive all year round, with ornamental flower buds and fine foliage. The leaves and branches are pleasantly aromatic when crushed. Flowers appear at different times depending on the climate, and it can spot flower throughout the year. Plant it as a feature in the garden so the stunning flowers can be on full display. Prune it very sparingly after flowering, taking care not to remove the next season's flower buds. **Climate:** Cool to warm temperate, Mediterranean. **Soil:** Moist to well-drained; loamy or sandy.

119. *Melaleuca linariifolia* 'Little Red'

1–1.2 m
1–1.2 m

A beautiful feature plant, this shrub has deep red new growth as well as small white flowers appearing in summer. It makes a lovely addition to the garden for the foliage, and the flowers also provide nectar for wildlife. It has a dense and neat habit, but it can also be pruned to the desired shape and to produce flushes of new red foliage. Adaptable to a range of soil types and situations, it does best in a soil with organic matter added and good drainage. **Climate:** Cool, cool to warm temperate, Mediterranean. **Soil:** Moist to well-drained; loamy or sandy, poor soil.

120. *Melaleuca nesophila* (showy honey myrtle)

2–5 m
1.5–4 m

This is an excellent ornamental with bright purplish pink pompom flowers in spring and summer. It has a long flowering period, providing a good source of nectar for wildlife. Growing to a medium shrub, it can be pruned to maintain a more compact shape. It has small aromatic leaves and a dense habit that provides shelter for small birds and other wildlife. It is easy to care for and doesn't have any significant pests or diseases. Originating from Western Australia, it is adaptable to a range of climates including coastal and inland regions. **Climate:** Cool, cool to warm temperate, Mediterranean. **Soil:** Well-drained; loamy or sandy, poor soil.

1–1.2 m

1–2 m

121. *Melaleuca thymifolia* (thyme-leaf honey myrtle)

Growing to a dense shrub, this plant features delicate, fringed, purple flowers throughout the year. There are also forms that have white or pink flowers. The crushed leaves have a spicy aroma. It can be used as a feature plant in a container or a small shrub for native gardens, or planted as a low hedge or screen. A tough and adaptable plant, it can tolerate both moist and dry soils and is mostly free of pests and diseases. The flowers attract nectar-eaters. **Climate:** Cool, cool to warm temperate, Mediterranean, subtropical. **Soil:** Moist to well-drained; loamy or sandy, poor soil.

0.2–0.4 m

0.2–0.5 m

122. *Mentha satureioides* (native pennyroyal)

A relative of culinary mint, the native pennyroyal is a perennial herb with a fragrance similar to peppermint. It can be used in place of culinary mint to flavour dishes and to make herbal tisanes. Similar to other types of mint, it sends out runners and is quite fast growing, so it should be grown in a pot to keep it from spreading. Native to most states of Australia, it thrives in damp shady areas but is adaptable to a range of conditions. **Climate:** Cool to warm temperate, Mediterranean, subtropical. **Soil:** Moist to well-drained; loamy or sandy.

0.2–0.5 m

0.2–0.3 m

123. *Microseris lanceolata* (yam daisy)

The yam daisy is native to southern parts of Australia and was once widespread in that region. The underground tubers are edible and were an important source of food for First Nations peoples in southern Australia until the introduction of sheep farming. The plant looks a lot like a dandelion, with a rosette of dark leaves plus yellow flowers. It is adaptable to a range of soils and conditions, but a bit of extra care will produce healthier plants and tubers. The tubers grow through summer and are ready to harvest in autumn. **Climate:** Cool, cool to warm temperate, Mediterranean, semi-arid. **Soil:** Moist to well-drained; loamy or sandy.

2–2.5 m

1–2 m

124. *Myoporum floribundum* (slender myoporum)

A graceful large shrub with a weeping habit and long slender leaves, this plant is highly ornamental. The leaves hang down from the branches, accentuating the weeping effect. Small white flowers cover the branches in the warmer months, attracting insects and birds to the garden. The perfumed flowers are so abundant that it looks as if snow is covering the branches. Tolerant of drought and frost once established, it is suited to a sheltered position in part-shade to full sun. **Climate:** Cool, cool to warm temperate, Mediterranean. **Soil:** Well-drained; loamy or sandy.

1.5–2 m

1–1.5 m

125. *Ozothamnus diosmifolius* 'Springtime White'

This is a low-maintenance ornamental that is tolerant of drought. It has abundant pure white flowers arranged in clusters. Best picked when still in bud, cut flowers last well in the vase; they can also be dried to prolong their life. Cutting the flowers will also help to prune the plant. It prefers a light well-drained soil and can be planted in raised beds or containers to provide the ideal conditions. **Climate:** Cool to warm temperate, Mediterranean, semi-arid, subtropical. **Soil:** Moist to well-drained; loamy or sandy, poor soil.

3–8 m

3–5 m

126. *Pandorea pandorana* 'Ruby Belle'

'Ruby Belle' is a lovely form of this native vine, featuring clusters of maroon-and-cream bell flowers in winter and spring. The deep green foliage is also attractive. A vigorous climber, it is useful for covering trellises and fences or creating secluded spaces in the garden. It also has a vigorous root system so should be situated away from drains and pipes. Plant it in an open, full-sun position with ample room to climb. It can be pruned to the desired size and shape. **Climate:** Cool to warm temperate, Mediterranean, subtropical. **Soil:** Moist to well-drained; loamy or sandy.

↑ 0.4–0.6 m
↔ 0.3–0.5 m

127. *Patersonia occidentalis* (native iris)

A great choice for drought-tolerant and cottage gardens, the native iris is a lovely ornamental. It has dark green strappy leaves and delicate violet flowers in spring and early summer. A tough plant, it grows from a rhizome and is easy to maintain. It is good for container planting in courtyards and patios or for use in landscaping. Old plants can be pruned to stimulate new growth. **Climate:** Cool to warm temperate, Mediterranean. **Soil:** Well-drained, dry; loamy or sandy, poor soil.

↑ 1–1.2 m
↔ 0.7–1 m

128. *Pimelea ferruginea* (pink rice flower)

With attractive deep pink flowers on a low dense shrub, the pink rice flower makes a lovely addition to dry native and cottage gardens. The flowers are very small but densely clustered into flower heads that stand out from the deep green foliage. Flowering from early spring through to summer, it makes a wonderful feature plant, well suited to rockeries and container growing. It prefers full sun and a well-drained soil. Use a quality native fertiliser in spring, and prune off old flower heads to keep it looking good. **Climate:** Cool to warm temperate, Mediterranean, semi-arid. **Soil:** Well-drained; loamy or sandy.

↑ 1–1.2 m
↔ 0.7–1 m

129. *Pimelea rosea* 'Deep Dream'

This cultivar bears abundant magenta flowers in spring, set against light green foliage on a compact shrub. Highly ornamental in flower, it makes a lovely feature plant and attracts butterflies to the garden. Ideal for rockeries and pots, it can also be used as a border plant. It prefers a full-sun position with a well-drained soil. **Climate:** Cool to warm temperate, Mediterranean, subtropical. **Soil:** Well-drained; loamy or sandy.

↑ 0.3–1 m
↔ 0.4–1 m

130. *Prostanthera cuneata* (alpine mint bush)

The alpine mint bush has lovely dark green foliage and relatively large white flowers with coloured markings inside, appearing in summer and autumn. The small leaves have a pleasant minty aroma when crushed. The flowers are ornamental and rich in nectar, attracting bees and other insects to the garden. It is a low and compact shrub that is best grown in a moist well-drained soil. **Climate:** Cool, cool temperate. **Soil:** Moist to well-drained; loamy or sandy, poor soil.

↑ 0.4–2.5 m
↔ 0.4–1.5 m

131. *Prostanthera magnifica* (magnificent prostanthera)

A spectacular plant when in flower, this species of mint bush bears large two-toned flowers in mauve and deep pink. The flowers cover the plant in spring and summer, putting on a beautiful display. A small to medium shrub from Western Australia, it is suited to dry climates. It can also be cultivated in areas with higher humidity if it is grown in a large pot with good drainage, or grafted onto tougher rootstock. Grow it in a well-drained soil in full sun or light shade. **Climate:** Warm temperate, Mediterranean, semi-arid. **Soil:** Well-drained; loamy or sandy.

↑ 1.5–5 m
↔ 1.5–4 m

132. *Prostanthera ovalifolia* (oval-leaf mint bush)

A beautiful shrub with abundant flowers in spring, this mint bush is a lovely ornamental with aromatic foliage. Often the flowers will cover the entire plant, turning it into a wash of purple. A fast-growing plant, it should be pruned each year after flowering to maintain a bushy shape. It prefers a moist well-drained soil, sheltered from harsh summer sun. It wilts in dry conditions, so it is useful for showing when the soil is drying out. It will bounce back when given water. **Climate:** Cool to warm temperate, Mediterranean, subtropical. **Soil:** Moist to well-drained; loamy or sandy.

133. *Ptilotus exaltatus* (tall mulla mulla)

 0.5–1.2 m
 0.4–0.5 m

 L
 SpS

 1

The tall mulla mulla is a wonderful ornamental with soft pinkish purple flower heads appearing in spring and summer. The flower heads also make great cut flowers. Suited to drier climates, it is a tough and drought-tolerant plant, though it can be short lived. It can be treated as an annual and propagated from seed. Best planted in a well-drained soil in an open sunny position, it is great for mixed containers and rockeries. **Climate:** Warm temperate, Mediterranean, semi-arid. **Soil:** Well-drained; loamy or sandy.

134. *Pultenaea pedunculata* (matted bush pea)

 0.2–0.6 m
 1–3 m

 L
SpS

 1

An endangered species in New South Wales, this dense ground cover bears bright yellow (or sometimes orange) pea flowers. Flowering from early spring through to the middle of summer, it brings delightful colour to the garden throughout the warmer months. Occurring on a range of soils in the wild, it prefers a moist well-drained soil and some shade. It is tolerant of drought and frost once established. **Climate:** Cool to warm temperate, Mediterranean. **Soil:** Moist to well-drained; clayey, loamy or sandy, poor soil.

135. *Pycnosorus globosus*, syn. *Craspedia globosa* (billy buttons)

 0.3–1 m
0.2–0.5 m
SpS
1–2

This is a lovely yet tough ornamental with soft silvery leaves and distinctive golden ball-shaped flowers on tall thin stems. The cheerful flowers are excellent for floral arranging and can be dried, too. It prefers a moist well-drained soil in part-shade to full sun. It can also tolerate heavy soils, so it is useful for difficult spots in the garden. It is a good plant for coastal gardens, container growing or planting in small groups for effect. **Climate:** Cool, cool to warm temperate, Mediterranean. **Soil:** Moist to well-drained; loamy or sandy.

136. *Regelia velutina* (Barrens regelia)

 1–2.5 m
 1–2 m

 L
Sp

 1

A relative of *Melaleuca*, this large shrub has similar flowers with clustered stamens. The bird-attracting blooms are bright red (or sometimes yellow) and borne on the ends of the branches, making it a showy plant when in flower. Native to Western Australia, it is an excellent plant for drier climates and well-drained soils, but it is generally short lived in areas with humid summers. It is best grown in a well-drained soil in full sun or light shade. **Climate:** Cool to warm temperate, Mediterranean, semi-arid. **Soil:** Well-drained, dry; loamy or sandy, poor soil.

137. *Ricinocarpos cyanescens* (little wedding bush)

 1–3 m
1–2 m
SpS

A dense shrub with masses of white flowers in spring and summer, this is a lovely low-maintenance plant, especially for coastal gardens. Grow it as a low hedge or in a native flower garden in a full-sun position for maximum flowering. It is tolerant of drought once established and has a naturally compact growth habit, making it easy to care for. **Climate:** Cool to warm temperate, Mediterranean. **Soil:** Moist to well-drained, dry; loamy or sandy, poor soil, saline soil.

138. *Santalum acuminatum* (quandong)

 1–6 m
 1–2 m

L
S

 1

A tough ornamental tree, the quandong is a hemiparasitic plant that relies on nearby host plants for nutrients and water. It does not damage the host plants but lives in a community with them, its roots extending up to 10 metres. Use local native species as host plants around the tree – the more the better. It can be difficult to cultivate, but it is worthwhile. It is an attractive and drought-tolerant tree, with olive green lance-shaped leaves and bright red fruits that are highly prized and taste like a blend between peach and rhubarb. **Climate:** Arid, semi-arid, warm temperate. **Soil:** Well-drained; loamy or sandy, poor soil, saline soil.

0.4–0.5 m

0.4–1 m

139. *Scaevola aemula* (fairy fan flower) C

A great low shrub for coastal gardens, this plant has delicate fan-shaped flowers in shades of purple. It looks wonderful grown in pots or hanging baskets so it can cascade over the sides, or it can be grown as a tough ground cover in the garden. The flowers appear in spring and summer, and they attract birds and insects. Grow it in a well-drained soil with some supplementary water during hot weather, and give it some native fertiliser in the growing season. **Climate:** Cool to warm temperate, Mediterranean, subtropical. **Soil:** Moist to well-drained; loamy or sandy.

0.4–0.5 m

1–2 m

140. *Scaevola calendulacea* (dune fan flower) C D E S

The dune fan flower is an excellent ground cover and soil stabiliser for sandy soils, as well as being a lovely drought-tolerant ornamental plant. It bears soft blue fan flowers that are lightly scented, and the leaves are bright green and fleshy. The flowers are followed by dark purple berries, which are edible and loved by birds. A prostrate spreading plant, it is well suited to coastal areas and exposed locations, growing naturally in sand dunes along Australia's east coast. It's also a good choice for rockeries and hanging baskets. **Climate:** Cool to warm temperate, Mediterranean, subtropical. **Soil:** Well-drained; loamy or sandy, poor soil, saline soil.

0.5–1 m

0.5–1 m

141. *Spyridium scortechinii,* syn. *Cryptandra scortechinii* (cotton bush)

The cotton bush is an attractive low shrub with masses of soft cottony flowers through winter and spring. The rust-coloured flower buds and dark green foliage add to its ornamental appeal. It looks great in rockeries and native gardens, preferring full sun and a well-drained soil. It's a low-maintenance plant: simply prune the flowers to display inside and then trim lightly after flowering to keep it in good shape. **Climate:** Cool to warm temperate, Mediterranean. **Soil:** Well-drained; clayey, loamy or sandy.

0.5–2 m

1–3 m

142. *Swainsona formosa* (Sturt's desert pea) D

An iconic native flower from arid regions of Australia, Sturt's desert pea is a wonderful drought-tolerant ornamental. It is a low spreading plant with greyish leaves and red flowers (there are also pink and cream forms available). It has specific needs, such as excellent drainage and full sun, and requires little water once established. It is especially good to grow in containers with a free-draining potting mix, and hanging baskets work well, too. **Climate:** Arid, Mediterranean, semi-arid, warm temperate. **Soil:** Well-drained; sandy.

2.5–3 m

2–3 m

143. *Telopea speciosissima* x *oreades* 'Shady Lady Red'

This is a cross between two waratah species, which makes it a better garden plant while allowing it to retain the spectacular flowers. A medium to large shrub with leathery leaves, it features large red flower heads in spring. The flower heads last well when cut, making them ideal for floral arrangements. It is great for native flower gardens and rockeries, and can also be grown in large pots. Grow it in a well-drained acidic soil, sheltered from hot afternoon sun. Water well until established and during hot dry weather. **Climate:** Cool, cool to warm temperate, Mediterranean, subtropical. **Soil:** Well-drained; loamy or sandy.

0.2–0.3 m

1–3 m

144. *Tetragonia implexicoma* (bower spinach) C E S

A tough coastal plant with edible leaves and fruits, bower spinach grows naturally on sand dunes along the east coast of Australia. Good for stabilising sandy soils and preventing erosion in exposed areas, it forms a prostrate scrambling ground cover. The small yellow flowers appear from late winter to spring and are scented. After flowering, the plant forms pink to dark red fruits that are both ornamental and edible. The leaves are semi-succulent and can be cooked and eaten in the same way as spinach. **Climate:** Cool to warm temperate, Mediterranean, subtropical. **Soil:** Well-drained; loamy or sandy, poor soil, saline soil.

0.2–0.3 m
 1–3 m

145. *Tetragonia tetragonioides* (warrigal greens) **C E S**

Warrigal greens is a common plant along the Australian coast. It is an easy-care alternative to spinach and a great plant for bush-food gardens. A sprawling ground cover, it can be used to spill over the sides of containers or to cover bare areas in the garden. It prefers a moist well-drained soil and light shade to full sun. Propagate from seed for a continuous supply of greens, or let it self-seed in the garden. The leaves need to be blanched before eating. **Climate:** Cool to warm temperate, Mediterranean, subtropical. **Soil:** Moist to well-drained; loamy or sandy, poor soil, saline soil.

 0.5–1 m
0.5–0.75 m

146. *Tetratheca thymifolia* (black-eyed Susan)

This low shrub puts on a beautiful display when in flower, with the whole plant covered in small magenta bell flowers with black centres. Easy to grow, it is an excellent plant for containers. It is also good for cottage gardens, rockeries and borders. It prefers a well-drained soil and a sunny or lightly shaded position with protection from the hot summer sun. Prune lightly after flowering to maintain a bushy shape. **Climate:** Cool to warm temperate, subtropical. **Soil:** Moist to well-drained; loamy or sandy.

0.15–0.3 m
0.5–6 m

147. *Themeda triandra* 'Mingo' **D**

A prostrate form of kangaroo grass with ornamental blue-toned leaves, this plant makes a lovely and unusual ground cover or border plant. It bears reddish brown flowers and seed heads in summer that contrast well with the foliage. Adaptable to a range of soil types, it is a good low-maintenance ground cover for native gardens. It is tolerant of drought and can be planted in positions from part-shade to full sun. **Climate:** Cool to warm temperate, Mediterranean, subtropical. **Soil:** Well-drained, dry; clayey, loamy or sandy, poor soil.

0.2–0.4 m
0.3–1 m

148. *Thomasia pygmaea* (tiny thomasia)

An intriguing plant from Western Australia, this low-growing shrub has masses of small, lantern-shaped, pink flowers covered in red speckles from late winter to spring. It is difficult to maintain in climates with humid summers, but it is worth growing for its ornamental appeal. Perfect for dry regions, it needs a well-drained soil and light shade to full sun. It is well suited to growing in pots with a free-draining potting medium. Regular tip pruning will keep the plant in good shape. **Climate:** Cool, cool to warm temperate, Mediterranean. **Soil:** Well-drained; loamy or sandy, poor soil.

0.75–1.5 m
1–1.5 m

149. *Thryptomene saxicola* 'FC Payne' **D**

This compact low-growing shrub features abundant pink flowers on slightly arching branches, flowering over an extended period. The leaves are slender, bright green and pleasantly aromatic. The stems can be cut and used for floral arrangements. It makes a great low hedge or background plant in the garden, and the small flowers are attractive to wildlife. It also does well in pots. Plant it in a well-drained soil, preferably sandy. It does best in areas with low humidity, and tolerates some frost and drought once established. **Climate:** Cool to warm temperate, Mediterranean, subtropical. **Soil:** Well-drained; loamy or sandy.

0.3–0.4 m
0.3–0.4 m

150. *Wahlenbergia stricta* 'Blue Mist'

This is a beautiful double-flowered form of the native bluebell in a striking shade of royal blue. A clumping dwarf perennial with fine foliage, it is perfect for cottage and flower gardens. Adaptable to a range of soils, it looks wonderful as a border plant, in rockeries and anywhere its wonderful flowers can be appreciated. It also works well as a pot plant or in a hanging basket. **Climate:** Cool, cool to warm temperate, Mediterranean, semi-arid, subtropical. **Soil:** Moist to well-drained; loamy or sandy.

0.1–0.3 m

0.5–2 m

151. *Westringia fruticosa* 'Flat'n'Fruity'

A tough, compact, prostrate form of coastal rosemary, this is a useful plant for stabilising soils and controlling erosion as well as suppressing weeds. The small white flowers appear from spring to autumn, and they attract native bees and butterflies. Easy to care for, it needs only the occasional light pruning to remove any dead branches. Great for coastal gardens and growing on banks, it can grow in poor soils and is tolerant of drought. **Climate:** Cool, cool to warm temperate, Mediterranean, semi-arid, subtropical. **Soil:** Well-drained, dry; loamy or sandy, poor soil, saline soil.

2–3 m

2–3 m

152. *Westringia longifolia* 'Snow Flurry'

This is a tall cultivar that is excellent for hedging, screening and topiary work. It has attractive slender leaves and small white flowers in winter and spring. Very hardy and adaptable, it can tolerate coastal conditions such as wind and salt, as well as frost and drought. Grow it in light shade to full sun, in moist or dry soils. It is a tough yet easy-care plant that requires little maintenance to keep it in good shape. **Climate:** Cool to warm temperate, Mediterranean, semi-arid, subtropical. **Soil:** Moist to well-drained, dry; clayey, loamy or sandy, poor soil, saline soil.

2–3 m

1–2 m

153. *Xanthorrhoea glauca* (grass tree)

The grass tree is an iconic Australian plant that is well adapted to free-draining soils low in nutrients, so it is a great plant for drought-tolerant native gardens. It is a very ornamental plant, particularly when in flower, and is excellent for landscaping work or as a feature plant in the garden. It is slow growing but very easy to care for once established. It does not like root disturbance, so take care when transplanting. If planting in a container, add gravel or sand to improve drainage. For garden beds, plant it on top of a mound of free-draining soil. **Climate:** Cool to warm temperate, Mediterranean, semi-arid. **Soil:** Well-drained; loamy or sandy, poor soil.

2–3 m

2–3 m

154. *Xanthorrhoea quadrangulata* (Mount Lofty grass tree)

This species of grass tree is from South Australia and has blue-green spiky leaves on a low trunk. It flowers irregularly when mature, and the stunning spikes can reach 5 metres in height. Grass trees are naturally slow growing, but this species is one of the faster ones. It needs full sun and excellent drainage, and can be grown in a large container in a sandy or gravelly medium. Follow the general planting and care advice for *Xanthorrhoea glauca*, taking care with the roots when transplanting. **Climate:** Cool to warm temperate, Mediterranean, semi-arid. **Soil:** Well-drained; loamy or sandy.

0.2–0.5 m

0.2–0.5 m

155. *Xerochrysum bracteatum* (golden everlasting)

An excellent plant for flower gardens and cut flowers, the golden everlasting produces bright daisy flowers throughout the year, peaking in spring. There are many different forms of this plant, with flower colours ranging from pink to red and orange. The flowers last well when cut, and they can also be dried to last even longer. A fast-growing plant, it should be tip pruned regularly to maintain a dense form. Feed it annually with a good slow-release fertiliser. It prefers a consistent supply of water. **Climate:** Cool to warm temperate, Mediterranean. **Soil:** Well-drained; loamy or sandy.

EXOTIC PLANTS

156. *Agave attenuata* (foxtail agave)

A common succulent in gardens, the foxtail agave is very low maintenance and withstands drought very well. The plant forms a large rosette of fleshy pale blue-green leaves on the end of a thick stem. It can take up to ten years for the plant to flower, with the striking flower spike growing 3–4 metres tall. The spike bears masses of small cream flowers that attract nectar-eating birds and insects. It works well as a landscaping plant when placed in small groups, or as a feature plant in a low-maintenance garden. **Climate:** Arid, warm temperate, Mediterranean, semi-arid, subtropical. **Soil:** Well-drained; loamy or sandy, poor soil.

157. *Agave victoriae-reginae* (royal agave)

A highly ornamental succulent that is ideal as a feature plant, the royal agave forms a ball-shaped rosette of dark green fleshy leaves with a striking white border along the edges. The white margins and thick angled leaves give the plant a sculptural appearance, but it also has spines. A slow-growing and low-maintenance plant, it is well adapted to drought conditions and needs a free-draining soil as it does not tolerate wet feet. It blooms only once and will die after flowering, though it may produce offsets. **Climate:** Arid, cool to warm temperate, Mediterranean, semi-arid, subtropical. **Soil:** Well-drained; loamy or sandy, poor soil.

158. *Aloe vera* (aloe vera)

Known for the soothing properties of its gel, aloe vera is an excellent drought-tolerant garden plant. A succulent that can withstand dry conditions well, aloe vera grows as a clumping plant with thick fleshy leaves featuring serrated edges. While it does survive drought well, it will grow better if planted in a good soil and given consistent water. Plant it in a very free-draining soil in part-shade to full sun. It can be grown in containers or en masse as a landscaping plant. **Climate:** Arid, cool to warm temperate, Mediterranean, semi-arid, subtropical. **Soil:** Well-drained; loamy or sandy, poor soil.

159. *Aloysia citriodora*, syn. *Aloysia triphylla* (lemon verbena)

With soft lemon-scented leaves and fragrant, tiny, white flowers in spring and summer, lemon verbena is a delight to have in the garden. The leaves can be used for herbal teas and dried for drawer sachets, or just enjoy the fragrance in the garden. This shrub grows in most parts of Australia but doesn't cope well with frost. Tip prune in spring to maintain a bushy growth habit, and use the pruned leaves and flowers for floral arrangements or make a tea from the leaves. **Climate:** Cool to warm temperate, Mediterranean, semi-arid, subtropical. **Soil:** Well-drained; loamy or sandy.

160. *Arthropodium cirratum* (New Zealand rock lily)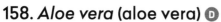

This is a great landscaping and foliage plant from New Zealand, perfect for shady positions with a dry soil. The large blue-green leaves create a lush tropical feel in the garden, and in spring it has spikes of small white flowers held above the foliage. Very tolerant of shade and drought, it is a useful plant for difficult spots in the garden. It also tolerates coastal conditions. It can be grown in containers or in a range of soil types, including poor and rocky soils. Great as an understorey plant, it is also useful for borders. **Climate:** Cool to warm temperate, Mediterranean, semi-arid, subtropical. **Soil:** Well-drained; loamy or sandy, poor soil.

161. *Borago officinalis* (borage)

Borage is a tough annual with delicate flowers that taste like cucumber and can be used to garnish dishes or added to drinks. Appearing throughout the year, the blue flowers develop a pinkish hue as they age, creating a lovely two-toned effect. Borage grows best in full sun but can handle some shade, and it prefers a moist well-drained soil. Grow in a sheltered position, protected from strong winds. It will self-seed readily in the garden. Plant near crops that need pollination, as it attracts bees. **Climate:** Cool, cool to warm temperate, Mediterranean, semi-arid. **Soil:** Moist to well-drained; loamy or sandy.

↑ 0.8–1 m
↔ 2–2.5 m

162. *Ceanothus 'Blue Cushion'* C D

A low-maintenance evergreen ground cover, this is great for sunny banks, rockeries and coastal gardens. Native to California, it has small dark green leaves and clusters of pale blue flowers in spring and summer. It requires little supplementary watering once established, but needs a well-drained soil and full sun for best flowering. The dense spreading habit makes it useful for suppressing weeds. Tolerant of drought, lime and moderate frost, it is a useful plant for ornamental gardens. It responds well to pruning. **Climate:** Cool to warm temperate, Mediterranean, subtropical. **Soil:** Well-drained; loamy or sandy.

↑ 0.8–1 m
↔ 1.5–1.8 m

163. *Chaenomeles japonica* (Japanese flowering quince) D

An ornamental deciduous shrub, the Japanese flowering quince is a tough and fast-growing species. It produces delicate red flowers in winter and spring. There are a number of cultivars with different coloured flowers, from cream to pink and scarlet. Low maintenance and hardy to drought and frost, it is a useful plant for hedging and screening as it has spiky branches. It can also be espaliered onto a wall or grown as a feature plant for its beautiful flowers. **Climate:** Cool to warm temperate, Mediterranean, semi-arid, subtropical. **Soil:** Well-drained; clayey, loamy or sandy.

↑ 2–5 m
↔ 1–4 m

164. *Citrus limon* 'Eureka' E

A popular variety of lemon, 'Eureka' flowers multiple times per year so is hardly ever without fruits. It produces fragrant lemons with plenty of juice. A great choice for containers, it prefers a moist well-drained soil but does not like wet feet. It has moderate water requirements but can withstand drier conditions once established. Great for warm-climate patios and courtyards, it is best situated in a sunny protected position out of strong winds. **Climate:** Cool to warm temperate, Mediterranean, subtropical. **Soil:** Moist to well-drained; clayey, loamy or sandy.

↑ 2–4 m
↔ 2–4 m

165. *Cotinus coggygria* (smoke bush)

The smoke bush is a beautiful shrub native to wide areas of Eurasia. It is deciduous, and the leaves go through a vibrant array of colours before dropping off. It is often used in floristry for its striking flower heads that resemble clouds of smoke, hence its common name. It is a highly ornamental shrub with a number of cultivars available, sporting different coloured leaves and flower heads. It does best in full sun and a well-drained soil. **Climate:** Cool to warm temperate, Mediterranean, semi-arid, subtropical. **Soil:** Well-drained; clayey, loamy or sandy.

↑ 3–4 m
↔ 3–4 m

166. *Cydonia oblonga* (quince) E

Grown as an ornamental as well as for its fruits, the quince is a tough and attractive tree with downy foliage. It needs cool winters to fruit well, and it can suffer fungal problems in areas with humid or wet summers. The fruits change from green to golden yellow when ripe, and this usually occurs in early to mid-autumn. Quince trees prefer a slightly acid soil, and a position sheltered from strong winds. Supplementary watering may be required in dry regions to ensure good fruit production. **Climate:** Arid, cool, cool to warm temperate, Mediterranean, semi-arid. **Soil:** Well-drained; clayey, loamy or sandy.

↑ 1–2 m
↔ 0.3–0.5 m

167. *Cynara scolymus* (globe artichoke) E

Grown as a vegetable or as an ornamental, the globe artichoke is an easy-care and rewarding plant to have in the water-smart garden. With a sculptural form as well as large mauve flowers resembling thistles, it is an attractive garden plant. Grow it in a well-drained soil enriched with organic matter, and give it plenty of space and a sheltered sunny position. It can be grown from seed in spring and will reach maturity quite quickly. The globe artichoke will form suckers that can be removed and used to propagate new plants. **Climate:** Cool, cool to warm temperate, Mediterranean, semi-arid. **Soil:** Well-drained; clayey, loamy or sandy.

0.5–1 m
0.5–1 m

168. *Echinocactus grusonii* (golden barrel cactus) Ⓓ

Native to Mexico, the golden barrel cactus is an easy-care plant that is perfect for growing in containers, as a house plant or in rockeries. It has a dark green central barrel covered in creamy yellow spines. Best in warmer climates, it is relatively fast growing and long lived, up to 30 years. Highly tolerant of drought, it can be watered every two weeks in summer but should be kept dry in winter. Water the soil and not the cactus, otherwise you will create an environment where the fungi that cause rot can thrive. **Climate:** Arid, warm temperate, Mediterranean, semi-arid, subtropical. **Soil:** Well-drained; loamy or sandy, potting mix.

1–2 m
1–2 m

169. *Echium candicans* (pride of Madeira) Ⓓ

A wonderful architectural plant, the pride of Madeira has a sculptural form and stunning flowers, and it is also highly tolerant of drought. It features grey-green foliage and large spikes of deep bluish purple flowers in the warmer months. The flowers are highly attractive to nectar-eating birds and insects. It is an excellent feature plant for dry climates and can be grown in a large container. It has become invasive in parts of Victoria, so check with local authorities before planting. **Climate:** Arid, cool, cool to warm temperate, Mediterranean, semi-arid, subtropical. **Soil:** Well-drained; clayey, loamy or sandy.

0.5 m
0.5–1 m

170. *Erigeron karvinskianus* (seaside daisy) Ⓢ

A prolific flowerer, the seaside daisy is a charming ground cover with a trailing growth habit, perfect for cottage gardens. Throughout most of the year, it produces white daisy flowers that age to pink. It self-seeds readily, but new plants can be removed if desired. It is a tough plant that will survive in almost any position, popping up between rocks and pavers. It looks great planted in containers where it will cascade over the sides. Prune after flowering to encourage a compact growth habit. **Climate:** Cool, cool to warm temperate, Mediterranean, semi-arid, subtropical. **Soil:** Well-drained; clayey, loamy or sandy, poor soil, saline soil.

0.5–2 m
0.5 m

171. *Ferocactus pilosus* (Mexican lime cactus)

A striking ornamental, this cactus has a central green barrel covered in bright red spines. Native to Mexico, it prefers a warm dry climate and can also be kept indoors. When growing outdoors in cooler climates, do not let the soil become cold and wet in winter, as this can lead to the growth of fungi. The cactus produces orange-and-red flowers in a ring around the top of the barrel in spring and summer, but it does not flower often in cultivation. It is best grown in containers, or in raised beds and rockeries. **Climate:** Arid, warm temperate, Mediterranean, semi-arid, subtropical. **Soil:** Well-drained; loamy or sandy, potting mix.

2–3 m
2–4 m

172. *Ficus carica* (fig) Ⓓ Ⓔ

The fig has long been cultivated for its fruits, and it is also a very ornamental and drought-tolerant tree. With its distinctive foliage and spreading form, it is a beautiful tree to have in the garden. It can be grown in most parts of Australia and prefers a Mediterranean climate with hot dry summers. It can easily be grown in containers and kept to a smaller size by pruning. The fig is deciduous in cooler climates but can retain its leaves in warmer areas. The fruits appear in late summer to early autumn, and the insignificant flowers are actually found inside the fruits. **Climate:** Arid, cool to warm temperate, Mediterranean, semi-arid, subtropical. **Soil:** Well-drained; clayey, loamy or sandy.

0.3–0.8 m
0.2–0.5 m

173. *Geranium phaeum* (dusky cranesbill) Ⓓ

A lovely ornamental for cottage gardens and difficult spots, this free-flowering geranium is a superb choice for water-smart gardens. It produces dark purple flowers through spring and summer, and sometimes at other times of the year. As well as being a great border plant and ground cover, it can be planted in groups under trees. It can be grown in a well-drained soil in deep shade, but prefers some sun. Tolerant of drought and frost, this useful evergreen perennial attracts pollinators. **Climate:** Cool, cool to warm temperate, Mediterranean, semi-arid, subtropical. **Soil:** Well-drained; clayey, loamy or sandy.

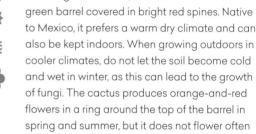

168

169

170

171

172

173

174

175

176

177

178

179

174. *Haemanthus coccineus* (paintbrush lily)

0.3–0.6 m

0.5–0.8 m

The paintbrush lily is an unusual and striking ornamental that produces prominent scarlet flowers in the warmer months, before the leaves appear. The brush-like flowers are borne on short, thick, brown stems around 30 centimetres tall. The dark green strappy leaves appear in autumn after the flowers have died down. A very drought-hardy plant, it is native to southern Africa and can grow in a poor soil with little water. It doesn't need supplementary watering unless conditions are very dry. Divide the bulbs to propagate new plants. **Climate:** Cool to warm temperate, Mediterranean, semi-arid. **Soil:** Well-drained; loamy or sandy.

175. *Hyacinthoides hispanica* (Spanish bluebell)

0.2–0.4 m

0.2–0.4 m

Related to the English bluebell, the tougher Spanish bluebell is better suited to Australian conditions but does not have scented flowers. It commonly has pale blue bell-shaped flowers, but there are also pink and white forms available. The flowers can be cut to display in vases. It naturalises easily, so make sure to keep plants contained to the desired areas. Alternatively, grow it in a container, as it makes a great pot plant, too. A rich well-drained soil in part-shade is ideal, and it can be mass planted underneath trees. **Climate:** Cool to warm temperate, Mediterranean, semi-arid. **Soil:** Well-drained; loamy or sandy.

176. *Laurus nobilis* (bay tree)

8–12 m

1–10 m

A well-known culinary and ornamental plant, the bay tree is excellent for drought-tolerant gardens. With low maintenance needs, it is a slow-growing evergreen tree that can be pruned to any desired shape. The dark green, glossy, aromatic leaves are used in cooking, particularly Mediterranean dishes. A great container plant, it can be kept at a small size by pruning. It can withstand temperatures down to around –5 degrees Celsius, and potted plants can be brought inside during winter. **Climate:** Cool, cool to warm temperate, Mediterranean, semi-arid, subtropical. **Soil:** Well-drained; clayey, loamy or sandy.

177. *Lavandula angustifolia* (English lavender)

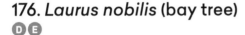

0.5–1 m

1–1.5 m

English lavender is well known as an aromatic herb, and its drought tolerance is excellent. With grey-green foliage and tall flower spikes in spring and summer, English lavender makes a great addition to any water-smart garden. It is a tough plant, withstanding both frosts and dry conditions. It does not like to be in a moist or heavy soil, so ensure that it is planted in a well-drained soil or placed in a raised bed if you have a heavy soil. Give it a light prune regularly to remove dead flower heads and promote new growth. **Climate:** Cool, cool to warm temperate, Mediterranean, semi-arid. **Soil:** Well-drained; loamy or sandy.

178. *Lavandula dentata* (French lavender)

0.5–1 m

0.5–1 m

Also known as toothed lavender, French lavender is a pretty ornamental that withstands tough conditions. It features soft grey-green foliage and tall flower spikes in spring and summer. Like other lavenders, it prefers a well-drained soil and full sun. French lavender is a beautiful plant for cottage gardens and flower gardens. It works well as a border, in containers and along pathways where the scent can be enjoyed. **Climate:** Cool, cool to warm temperate, Mediterranean, semi-arid. **Soil:** Well-drained; loamy or sandy.

179. *Leucospermum* 'Carnival Red'

1–1.5 m

1–1.5 m

Known as pincushions, *Leucospermum* is a genus from southern Africa, and the plants have similar needs to Australian natives. This *Leucospermum* cultivar has a compact growth habit and features abundant bright red pincushion flowers in spring. It is a low-maintenance shrub that tolerates drought and light frost once established. It needs a well-drained soil in light shade to full sun. If planting it in a pot, use a potting mix designed for natives. The flowers attract birds and can be used as cut flowers. **Climate:** Arid, cool to warm temperate, Mediterranean, semi-arid. **Soil:** Well-drained; loamy or sandy.

180. *Limonium perezii* (sea lavender)

A tough perennial from the Canary Islands, sea lavender has glossy green leaves. Purple flower heads appear throughout the warmer months. The flowers are borne high above the foliage on long stems. It is a low-growing plant, good for borders and rockeries. It is tolerant of drought and light frost, and withstands coastal conditions well. The flower heads can be cut for fresh or dried flower arrangements, and they keep their colour well. **Climate:** Cool, cool to warm temperate, Mediterranean, semi-arid. **Soil:** Well-drained; loamy or sandy.

181. *Morus nigra* (black mulberry)

The black mulberry is a beautiful ornamental tree, and it also bears delicious edible fruits. It is a large, deciduous, spreading tree with pendulous branches that can reach down to the ground. Grow it in a moist soil rich in organic matter in a full-sun position. It grows well in most areas except tropical climates. Tolerant of drought, it does appreciate some extra water in summer. Prune it hard in winter to keep the tree at an accessible size. **Climate:** Cool, cool to warm temperate, Mediterranean, semi-arid. **Soil:** Moist to well-drained; clayey, loamy or sandy.

182. *Ocimum kilimandscharicum* (camphor basil)

This basil species from eastern Africa provides nectar-filled flowers all year round that are magnets for bees and other pollinators. The evergreen leaves have a strong camphor aroma and can be used for tea and medicinal baths, and as an insect repellent. It is a great perennial herb for water-smart gardens. **Climate:** Cool to warm temperate, Mediterranean, semi-arid, subtropical. **Soil:** Well-drained; loamy or sandy.

183. *Pelargonium crispum* (lemon geranium)

The lemon geranium comes from South Africa and has small, crinkled, scented leaves and small light pink flowers. Well suited to borders, container growing and cottage gardens, it should be placed where the scent can be enjoyed. It is best grown in full sun, and this also encourages more flowering. Reduce watering in winter, as it prefers good drainage. It can be pruned back quite hard in autumn and spring. The leaves can be used to make potpourri and to flavour desserts. **Climate:** Cool to warm temperate, Mediterranean, semi-arid. **Soil:** Well-drained; loamy or sandy.

184. *Pelargonium tomentosum* (peppermint geranium)

The peppermint geranium has velvety green leaves that have a pleasant mint aroma when crushed. Ensure that it has some afternoon shade; a position in part-shade is ideal. It has a somewhat trailing habit and looks good in hanging baskets or cascading down an embankment. It is not as tolerant of drought as other *Pelargonium* species, but it can withstand dry periods once established. The leaves can be used in potpourri or to flavour drinks and desserts. **Climate:** Cool to warm temperate, Mediterranean. **Soil:** Moist to well-drained; loamy or sandy.

185. *Protea cynaroides* (king protea)

The king protea comes from South Africa but has similar cultivation requirements to Australian natives such as banksias. Proteas are adapted to poor soils, so they are suited to Australian growing conditions. The king protea is a small to medium shrub with prominent flower heads in late winter and spring. The showy flower heads attract birds, and they last well in floral arrangements. There are cultivars available with white, pink and red flower heads. Tolerant of dry conditions once established, it can also withstand light frosts. **Climate:** Cool to warm temperate, Mediterranean, semi-arid, subtropical. **Soil:** Well drained; loamy or sandy.

180

181

182

183

184

185

186. *Prunus dulcis*, syn. *Prunus amygdalus* (almond)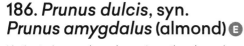

Native to Iran and nearby regions, the almond is an attractive deciduous tree with beautiful blossoms in spring. A shrubby small to medium tree, it is also available in dwarf varieties that can be grown in containers. Many varieties need a male and female tree to set fruit, but self-pollinating forms are also available (which means you only need to grow one tree to produce fruits). Almonds grow best in a climate with cool winters as well as dry summers and autumns. Trees can start producing fruits from the third year. **Climate:** Arid, cool to warm temperate, Mediterranean, semi-arid. **Soil:** Well-drained; loamy or sandy.

187. *Punica granatum* (pomegranate)

The pomegranate has been in cultivation for a long time, and it is grown both for its fruits and as an ornamental plant. There are varieties grown for hedging that do not produce fruits. The pomegranate is deciduous or semi-deciduous, depending on the climate. Position the shrub or small tree in full sun, in a growing mix enriched with organic matter, and ensure that it has adequate water in spring, during flowering and fruiting. Aside from that, it is a drought-tolerant plant. **Climate:** Arid, cool to warm temperate, Mediterranean, semi-arid, subtropical. **Soil:** Well-drained; clayey, loamy or sandy.

188. *Romneya coulteri* (Californian tree poppy)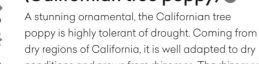

A stunning ornamental, the Californian tree poppy is highly tolerant of drought. Coming from dry regions of California, it is well adapted to dry conditions and grows from rhizomes. The rhizomes spread underground very easily, so keep this in mind when planting. The foliage is grey-green, and the large flowers have crinkled white petals and large yellow stamens in the centre. The plant is very showy when in flower. It thrives in summer heat and dry sandy soils, so plant it in full sun in a freely draining position. **Climate:** Arid, cool, cool to warm temperate, Mediterranean, semi-arid. **Soil:** Well-drained; loamy or sandy, poor soil.

189. *Rosa banksiae* (Banks' rose)

Native to central and western China, this is a tough and vigorous rose with few thorns. It is evergreen or semi-deciduous, depending on the climate, and bears small, scented, white or pale yellow flowers. It has a climbing habit and is great for growing over fences, trellises or archways. Plant it in a rich soil, and water consistently while it is becoming established. It prefers a position in full sun in order to flower at its best. Prune lightly after flowering to shape the plant. It is one of the earliest roses to flower, starting in early spring. **Climate:** Cool, cool to warm temperate, Mediterranean, subtropical. **Soil:** Well-drained; clayey, loamy or sandy.

190. *Rosmarinus officinalis*, syn. *Salvia rosmarinus* (rosemary)

Rosemary is a great drought-tolerant herb as well as an excellent ornamental. The thin dark green leaves are white underneath, and the plant forms a small shrub with woody stems. Small lavender-coloured flowers appear from autumn to spring in temperate climates. In warmer climates, it can flower all year. It can be used for landscaping as well as in the herb garden, and it does well in pots. Pests do not bother it. **Climate:** Arid, cool, cool to warm temperate, Mediterranean, semi-arid, subtropical. **Soil:** Well-drained; clayey, loamy or sandy, poor soil.

191. *Salvia apiana* (white sage)

Native to the dry regions of the south-western United States (where it is an important plant for First Nations peoples) and north-western Mexico, the white sage is a tough ornamental plant with aromatic leaves. It is used to make 'smudge sticks' and is often illegally harvested from the wild for this purpose. The plant has long silvery leaves and thrives in hot dry conditions. Water deeply and infrequently, and do not let the leaves get wet. It can become invasive in the right climate, so check with local authorities before planting it. **Climate:** Arid, cool to warm temperate, Mediterranean, semi-arid. **Soil:** Well-drained; loamy or sandy, poor soil.

1.5–2 m

1–1.5 m

192. *Salvia canariensis* (Canary Island sage)

This sage can withstand cooler conditions than most and has lance-shaped leaves with a soft silvery down. The flowers are lilac with burgundy calyces underneath, giving a two-toned effect. Tough in hot summers, it also tolerates moderate frosts. It prefers a full-sun position in a well-drained soil. Some supplementary water will help the plant to grow larger. It can be pruned in late winter to keep it in shape. The flowers attract bees and other insects to the garden. **Climate:** Cool, cool to warm temperate, Mediterranean, semi-arid. **Soil:** Well-drained; loamy or sandy.

0.5–0.8 m

0.8–1 m

193. *Salvia officinalis* (sage) E

Sage is well known to gardeners who like to cook, as it is used as a culinary herb. A great water-smart plant, it prefers a full-sun position in a well-drained soil. The leaves are covered in soft hairs and are silvery green, while the tubular flowers are bluish purple. There is also a form with purple leaves. Sage is a great bee attractant for the garden, and all parts of the plant are fragrant. It is well adapted to hot dry conditions, so do not allow the roots to become waterlogged. **Climate:** Arid, cool, cool to warm temperate, Mediterranean, semi-arid. **Soil:** Well-drained; loamy or sandy.

1–1.5 m

0.8–1 m

194. *Salvia yangii*, syn. *Perovskia atriplicifolia* (Russian sage) C

Russian sage is an ornamental that can withstand dry conditions. It has grey-green leaves and bluish violet flowers on tall spires. It is a good plant for coastal gardens, as it likes a full-sun position and can tolerate a variety of soils, from heavy clay to light sandy soil. It is a low-maintenance plant that does not like too much water or fertiliser. It can spread via underground rhizomes beyond the original planting area; if this is a concern, grow it in a container. **Climate:** Arid, cool, cool to warm temperate, Mediterranean, semi-arid, subtropical. **Soil:** Well-drained; clayey, loamy or sandy.

0.5–0.6 m

0.3 m

195. *Santolina chamaecyparissus* (cotton lavender)

Native to the Mediterranean, cotton lavender has grey-green foliage and yellow ball-shaped flowers. It looks great planted with Australian natives and other plants with silvery foliage, and is superb planted in groups or used as a border. The leaves are strongly scented and can be used to make herbal insect repellents. Water consistently during the warmer months and deadhead the flowers regularly. It does not tolerate having wet roots in winter. **Climate:** Arid, cool, cool to warm temperate, Mediterranean, semi-arid, subtropical. **Soil:** Well-drained; clayey, loamy or sandy.

1–2 m

1–2 m

196. *Strelitzia reginae* (bird of paradise) C D

A popular ornamental plant originally from South Africa, the bird of paradise is tough and striking in appearance. The large dark leaves and brightly coloured flowers give the plant a tropical look, and it can handle drought and coastal conditions. Once established, it is very low maintenance, but the leaves will take on a darker green hue if the plant is given more water. In drier conditions, the leaves have a silvery sheen. The showy blooms make great cut flowers, and deadheading will encourage the plant to flower a lot more. **Climate:** Cool to warm temperate, Mediterranean, semi-arid, subtropical. **Soil:** Well-drained; loamy or sandy.

0.5–1.2 m

0.5–1.2 m

197. *Teucrium fruticans* (shrubby germander) C

Shrubby germander is an attractive ornamental in the mint family. It grows as a low shrub with slightly arching woody branches. Small bluish lilac flowers appear in summer. The foliage is covered in silvery down that gives it an almost white appearance. It needs excellent drainage and full sun, and it is good for coastal gardens. Great for landscaping, it needs little water once established. It is low maintenance, only needing a light prune after flowering to keep it in shape. **Climate:** Arid, cool, cool to warm temperate, Mediterranean, semi-arid. **Soil:** Well-drained; loamy or sandy, poor soil.

192

193

194

195

196

197

198

0.2–0.3 m
0.5–1 m

198. *Thymus vulgaris* (thyme) D E

Thyme is a low spreading herb with tiny round leaves that are used in cooking and herbal remedies. It is a tough evergreen plant that withstands drought well but can be short-lived; fortunately, it can be propagated easily from cuttings. The plant has tiny purple (or sometimes pink) flowers in summer. It makes a good ground cover, and is great planted in rockeries and containers. There are many varieties and related species of thyme with slightly different scents, such as lemon thyme. **Climate:** Arid, cool, cool to warm temperate, Mediterranean, semi-arid, subtropical. **Soil:** Well-drained; loamy or sandy, poor soil.

199

2–5 m
2–5 m

199. *Vitis vinifera* (grape vine) D E

The grape vine is a deciduous climber, and there are many varieties available for wine-making, table grapes, vine leaves and ornamental uses. The right variety should be selected for your climate. Some do not like humidity, while others can tolerate it well. It is generally quite a drought-tolerant plant, but for fruit production more consistent watering will be required. The grape is great for covering patios and pergolas, as it lets sun through in winter and gives shade in summer. Frost tolerance depends on the variety grown. **Climate:** Cool, cool to warm temperate, Mediterranean, semi-arid, subtropical. **Soil:** Well-drained; clayey, loamy or sandy.

200

2–8 m
2–8 m

200. *Wisteria sinensis* (Chinese wisteria) D

Chinese wisteria is a vigorous deciduous vine with a beautiful spring floral display of scented pendulous flowers on bare branches. The flowers are usually lavender, but they can range from white to pink or purple. It is a tough plant that withstands drought once established, and it appreciates a well-drained soil rich in organic matter. For best flowering, plant it in a sheltered position in full sun. It needs a good support structure as it has a vigorous growth habit, and it can be pruned as much as desired. **Climate:** Cool, cool to warm temperate, Mediterranean, semi-arid, subtropical. **Soil:** Well-drained; clayey, loamy or sandy.

INDEX

ACKNOWLEDGEMENTS

EMMA

I would like to thank my family for their support while writing the book, and particularly my little brother, Jack. I would also like to thank my dear friend, Carey Badcoe, who has supported and believed in me throughout this process.

A special thankyou is due to all of those at Murdoch Books who helped to bring this book to life during the chaotic circumstances of the pandemic, including Corinne Roberts, Jane Willson, Madeleine Kane, Vivien Valk, Dannielle Viera and Justin Wolfers. I appreciate your help and patience throughout.

Thanks also to photographer Brent Wilson for walking me through my first photo shoot and capturing my garden so well.

ANGUS

I would like to thank the wonderful team at Murdoch Books who worked so hard on this project, including Corinne Roberts, Jane Willson, Madeleine Kane, Vivien Valk, Dannielle Viera and Justin Wolfers.

I would also like to thank photographers and handypeople Kathrin Seels and Mark Seels for all of their help in creating and shooting various projects on the farm in Tasmania.

Thank you to those who provided some of the technologies and designs featured in the book, including Ian Collins from WaterUps for his innovative capillary-watering knowledge and products including the Sub-Irrigation Channel; Nigel and Hannah Nattrass of RELN and Tumbleweed for the supply of Stretch Ag-Pipe, worm farms and Gedye Compost Bins; Ryan Strating for letting us install and photograph the roof garden at Cascade House by Core Collective Architecture, and his other business Clinka for supplying expanded clay aggregates for the roof-garden project.

Also, Wendy Siu-Chew Lee from Up on the Rooftop for the supply of her fabulous Ollas and Terracotta Water Spikes; Jackie Hammond, David Anderson and Anton Lee See from Blue Mountain Co for the design and supply of their rainwater technologies; Premaydena Community Garden; Dr Richard Stirzaker and Matthew Driver of the CSIRO Virtual Irrigation Academy for the supply of their Chameleon Card System for monitoring soil moisture.

Lastly, and most importantly, I want to thank my wonderful partner, Mary-ann Materia, for all her love and support in helping me to bring my part in the book to completion through the Covid pandemic, a very difficult time for so many.

Published in 2022 by Murdoch Books,
an imprint of Allen & Unwin

Murdoch Books Australia
83 Alexander Street
Crows Nest NSW 2065
Phone: +61 (0)2 8425 0100
murdochbooks.com.au
info@murdochbooks.com.au

Murdoch Books UK
Ormond House
26–27 Boswell Street
London WC1N 3JZ
Phone: +44 (0) 20 8785 5995
murdochbooks.co.uk
info@murdochbooks.co.uk

For corporate orders and custom publishing, contact
our business development team at salesenquiries@
murdochbooks.com.au

Publisher: Corinne Roberts
Editorial Manager: Justin Wolfers
Design Manager: Vivien Valk
Designer: Madeleine Kane
Editor: Dannielle Viera
Photographers: Brent Wilson, Kathrin Seels
and Angus Stewart
Illustrator: Marcela Restrepo
Production Director: Lou Playfair

*We acknowledge that we meet and work on the traditional
lands of the Cammeraygal people of the Eora Nation and
pay our respects to their elders past, present and future.*

ISBN 9 781 92235 130 2 Australia
ISBN 9 781 91166 812 1 UK

A catalogue record for this
book is available from the
National Library of Australia

A catalogue record for this book is available from the
British Library

Colour reproduction by Splitting Image Colour Studio Pty Ltd,
Clayton, Victoria
Printed by C&C Offset Printing Co. Ltd., China

10 9 8 7 6 5 4 3 2 1

Cover photography, from front left: © Angus Stewart 2022;
© Kathrin Seels 2022; © Angus Stewart 2022; © Brent
Wilson 2022. Back cover: © Kathrin Seels 2022

Internal photography credits:
Photographs © Kathrin Seels 2022 pages 4–7, 10, 12, 26, 31,
34, 38, 43, 44, 46, 55, 56 (bottom left), 59, 63, 66, 67, 68 (left), 71,
72–73, 81 (right), 82–88, 90–95, 101 (top), 102–105, 107 (left), 109
(right), 110 (right), 111, 112 (left), 113 (right), 114–117, 120, 125, 128, 130
(top), 134, 136 (right), 137, 140–143, 147, 148–152, 156–159, 238, 247.

Photographs © Brent Wilson 2022 pages 11, 18, 25, 60, 65, 68
(right), 74–77, 81 (left), 89 (left), 101 (bottom), 131.

Photographs © Angus Stewart 2022 pages: 9, 10 (bottom left),
17, 21, 22–23, 24, 32 (right), 35, 37, 40–41, 42, 48, 49 (bottom left),
50–51, 56 (top and bottom right), 57, 69, 70, 78 (right) 99, 106,
107 (right), 108 (right), 109 (left), 110, 112 (right), 113 (left), 118, 119
(except for middle row, left, and bottom right), 121, 126–127, 130
(bottom), 133, 136 (left), 138 (top and bottom), 154–155, 160–161,
162–239 (excepting the below).

Additional photographs: page 2 © Shutterstock, by Alyba;
49 (bottom right) © Shutterstock, by Kira Yan; 78 (left)
© Airgarden; 89 (right) © Vegepod; 108 © Shutterstock, by
Jitlada Panwiset; 119 © Shutterstock, by Maciej Bledowski;
169 (bottom left) © iStock, by JackF; 174 (top left) © FlickR, by
Jean and Fred Hort; 176 (bottom right) © FlickR, by Forest
and Kim Starr; 178 (middle row, right) © iStock, by Anja
Hennern; 178 (bottom left) © Shutterstock, by Ken Griffiths;
181 (middle row, left) © Shutterstock, by Svetlana Zhukova;
182 (top right) © Shutterstock, by Ken Griffiths;
182 (middle row, right) © Shutterstock, by Siglinde Dinsdale;
182 (bottom left) © Shutterstock, by demamiel62; 185 (top
right) © Shutterstock, by Siglinde Dinsdale; 190 (middle
row, right); Shutterstock, by Wattlebird; 190 (bottom left)
© Shutterstock, by demamiel62; 193 (top right) © Shutterstock,
by Martin Fowler; 199 (top right): Wikipedia, by Stickpen;
201 (bottom left) © Shutterstock, by alybaba; 201 and 223
(bottom right) © Shutterstock, by Michael Willis; 202 (middle
row, left) © Shutterstock, by Anne Powell; 206 (middle row,
right) © Shutterstock, by Marta Kolotylo; 209 (top left)
© Shutterstock, by demamiel62; 218 (middle row, right)
© FlickR, by manuel m. v.; 223 (middle row, left) © Shutterstock,
by Viktorialvanets; 223 (bottom right) © Shutterstock, by Dario
Sabljak; 224 (bottom left) © Shutterstock, by darksoul72;
224 (bottom right) © Shutterstock, by Arina_B; 227 (top right)
© Shutterstock, by Dirk M. de Boer; 227 (bottom right)
© Shutterstock, by Alienor Llona Bonnard; 228 (top right)
© Shutterstock, by Kollawat Somsri; 228 (middle row, left)
© iStock, by pelvidge; 232 (bottom left) © Shutterstock,
by nnattalli.